Contents

OCCASIONAL PA 85

Thailand: Adjusting to Success
Current Policy Issues

David Robinson, Yangho Byeon, and Ranjit Teja
with Wanda Tseng

INTERNATIONAL MONETARY FUND
Washington DC
August 1991

Library of Congress Cataloging-in-Publication Data

Robinson, David, 1958–
Thailand : adjusting to success : current policy issues / by David Robinson, Yangho Byeon, and Ranjit Teja with Wanda Tseng.
p. cm. — (Occasional paper / International Monetary Fund, ISSN 0251-6365 ; 85)
Includes bibliographical references.
ISBN 1-55775-221-4
1. Thailand—Economic policy. 2. Fiscal policy—Thailand. 3. Finance—Thailand. 4. Thailand—Commercial policy. I. Byeon, Yangho, 1954– . II. Teja, Ranjit, 1958– . III. Title. IV. Series: Occasional paper (International Monetary Fund) ; no. 85.
HC445.R63 1991
338.9593—dc20 91-27934
CIP

Price: US$10.00
(US$7.50 to full-time faculty members and students at universities and colleges)

Please send orders to:
International Monetary Fund, Publication Services
700 19th Street, N.W., Washington, D.C. 20431, U.S.A.
Tel.: (202) 623-7430 Telefax: (202) 623-7201

The following symbols have been used throughout this paper:

... to indicate that data are not available;

— to indicate that the figure is zero or less than half the final digit shown, or that the item does not exist;

– between years or months (e.g., 1990–91 or January–June) to indicate the years or months covered, including the beginning and ending years or months;

/ between years (e.g., 1990/91) to indicate a crop or fiscal (financial) year.

"Billion" means a thousand million.

Minor discrepancies between constituent figures and totals are due to rounding.

The term "country," as used in this paper, does not in all cases refer to a territorial entity that is a state as understood by international law and practice; the term also covers some territorial entities that are not states, but for which statistical data are maintained and provided internationally on a separate and independent basis.

Preface

The 1991 Annual Meetings of the Board of Governors of the International Monetary Fund and the World Bank in Bangkok provide a good occasion for a review of Thailand's recent economic development and prospects. This paper is based largely on documentation prepared in connection with the 1991 Article IV consultation with Thailand.

The authors would like to acknowledge the assistance and warm hospitality extended to them by the Thai authorities, particularly the staff of the Bank of Thailand. They also wish to express their gratitude to P.R. Narvekar, who originally suggested the idea of an Occasional Paper, and to Linda M. Koenig, who directed the initial work; and to record their appreciation to Melanie Dieckman, Natalie Hairfield, and Noy Siackhachanh for research assistance, to Rosanne Heller of the Asian Department and to Elin Knotter of the External Relations Department for editorial comments and advice, and to Ollie Goodger, Florence Lee, and Molly Singh for secretarial support. While the paper has benefited from comments and suggestions both from the Thai authorities and from colleagues in the Fund and the World Bank, any opinions expressed are those of the authors alone and do not necessarily reflect the views of the Thai authorities, Executive Directors of the IMF, or other IMF staff members. The authors bear sole responsibility for any factual errors.

THAILAND
International boundaries
Regional boundaries
National capital
0 50 100 200 Miles
0 100 200 300 Kilometers
Chiang Rai
Chiang Mai
Lampang
NORTH
Phitsanulok
Nakhon Sawan
Udon Thani
Khon Kaen
NORTHEAST
Ubon Ratchathani
Nakhon Ratchasima
CENTRAL
Ayutthaya
Nakhon Pathom
BANGKOK
Ratchaburi
ANDAMAN SEA
Chumphon
GULF OF THAILAND
Nakhon Si Thammarat
Phuket
SOUTH
Hat Yai
India
China
Lao People's Dem. Rep.
Myanmar
Thailand
Cambodia
ANDAMAN SEA
Viet Nam
SOUTH CHINA SEA
Malaysia
Indonesia
Singapore

I Introduction

Thailand's economic performance over the past several decades is an excellent example of successful development, combining adjustment with growth. The achievements of the 1980s continue this record. Early in the decade, like many other developing countries, Thailand was hit hard by the global recession and the downturn in commodity prices. However, a prompt and pragmatic policy response restored macroeconomic balance and poised the economy to take full advantage of the improved international environment by 1986. Since then, spurred by rapid increases in investment and exports, Thailand has experienced a sustained economic boom that is spectacular even by the standards of a region renowned for its economic dynamism. While Thailand's recent success can be attributed to many factors, three in particular predominate: a commitment to an outward-oriented, market-based economic system; a development strategy centered on the private sector; and a tradition of cautious financial policies.

The success of Thailand's recent economic performance has, however, led to increasing strains on the economy, manifested in the emergence of infrastructural bottlenecks, a sharp increase in the current account deficit, and a pickup in inflation. The challenge facing policymakers now is how best to sustain the momentum of the economy while keeping demand pressures in check. This in turn will require measures to reduce a variety of structural impediments to growth. In particular, the need for substantial infrastructural investment in both physical and human capital is widely recognized, and, to support this, a strengthening of domestic savings is required. The deregulation of domestic markets is seen as essential to improve economic efficiency and enhance the potential for growth, particularly in the areas of tax reform, liberalization of the financial system, and tariff reduction. At the same time, policymakers have increasingly stressed the need to improve the quality of growth, which has been adversely affected by both environmental problems and a deterioration in income distribution. This paper addresses some of these current policy issues.

The next section provides an overview of Thailand's postwar economic development, outlining the reasons for its economic success and the main policy issues facing the authorities. The paper then focuses on the role of fiscal policy, reviewing the fiscal adjustment of the 1980s and considering the implications of infrastructural investment and tax reform for fiscal policy in the 1990s. Next it discusses plans for liberalization of the financial sector designed to boost domestic savings to support future growth, to enhance its ability to compete in international markets, and ultimately to develop Thailand as a regional financial center. The paper then examines the need for tariff reform to reduce the level and dispersion of effective protection and improve the efficiency of investment. The final section sets Thailand's economic development in a regional context, assessing both the commonality of experience in Thailand, Indonesia, and Malaysia, and the role that the region has played in these three countries' recent economic success.

Box I. A Profile of Thailand

Thailand, literally the "Land of the Free," is situated in the western part of the Indochinese peninsula, bordered by Myanmar, the Lao People's Democratic Republic, Cambodia, and Malaysia. The Thai people migrated southward and westward from China around the tenth century A.D., although archaeological evidence indicates that the area has been inhabited almost continuously for the last 20,000 years. With an area of about 513,000 square kilometers—a little smaller than France—the country can be divided broadly into four regions: the cool and mountainous North, comprising a series of steep mountain ranges incised by steep valleys and rivers; the semiarid Northeast; the fertile central plain, chiefly consisting of the Chao Phraya River delta; and the densely forested southern isthmus. The climate is tropical and cool, with high temperatures and humidity: the rainy season is June–October, the cool season, November–February, and the hot season, March–May.

Since 1932, Thailand has been a constitutional monarchy. The monarch, currently King Bhumibol Adulyadej, is the head of state and commander of the armed forces. The head of government is the Prime Minister, appointed by the king on the advice of the National Assembly. The military has traditionally played a major role in Thailand's political life: in February 1991, the civilian government headed by Prime Minister Chatichai Choonhaven was overthrown in a military coup and replaced by the military-dominated National Peacekeeping Council (NPC). In early March, the NPC appointed an interim government headed by Prime Minister Anand Panyarachun and consisting primarily of civilians, in advance of elections scheduled to be held in the first half of 1992.

Thailand has a population of about 56 million, with population growth averaging about 2 percent a year during the 1980s. Almost one half of the population is Thai, with sizable Lao, Chinese, and Malay minorities: 99 percent of the population is Buddhist, while the remainder includes Moslems, Hindus, Sikhs, and Christians. Despite heavy rural to urban migration, only 19 percent of the population lives in urban areas, of which almost half live in and around Bangkok, now the fourteenth largest city in the world.

Thailand is generously endowed with natural resources. About 40 percent of the total land area is cultivated, and some 29 percent is under forest. Rice remains the staple cash crop, although its dominance has declined in recent years: other major crops include maize, sugar, tapioca, rubber, tobacco, bananas, pineapples, and kenaf (a jute-like fiber). Until the ban on commercial logging (see Box 4), Thailand was also a major producer of timber, particularly teak. Thailand's mineral resources include tin, brown coal, iron, and manganese, with substantial deposits of sapphires, rubies, and other gems. There are also considerable reserves of natural gas (which now accounts for nearly one third of Thailand's energy needs) and, to a lesser extent, crude oil.

Thailand's per capita income of $1,454 (1990) places it in the ranks of lower middle-income countries. Although 60 percent of the population still earns its living from agriculture, growth in recent years has increasingly come from industry and services, which now account for more than 80 percent of GDP. Manufacturing output, formerly dominated by agroindustrial production and textiles, has become increasingly diversified, with especially rapid growth in the production of construction materials, transport equipment, electrical appliances and components, and machinery and equipment. The financial sector, although still relatively underdeveloped, has expanded rapidly; and, with the number of foreign visitors more than tripling, to over 5 million during the 1980s, Thailand has also become an important tourist destination.

Table 1. Social Indicators

GDP per capita (*current U.S. dollars, 1990*)	1,454
Population and vital statistics	
Total population (*in millions; 1990*)	56.08
Population growth (*annual growth; in percent*)	2[1]
Urban population (*percent*)	19
Life expectancy at birth (*years*)	
Overall	67
Female	69
Crude birth rate (*per thousand*)	21
Crude death rate (*per thousand*)	6
Infant mortality rate (*per thousand; 1987*)	11
Labor force (*1989*)	
Total labor force (*in millions*)	30.3
Employed work force (*in millions*)	29.2
Agriculture (*percent of total*)	60.1
Manufacturing (*percent of total*)	10.4
Public health and education	
Population per physician (*1988*)	4,985
Population per nurse (*1988*)	1,692
Adult literacy rate (*percent; 1985*)	91
Primary school enrollment (*percent; 1985*)	95

Sources: Data provided by the Thai authorities; and World Bank, *Social Indicators of Development, 1990.*
[1]Over the period 1980–90.

Table 2. Summary Data, 1985–90

86-90 9.92 "AVG GDP GROWTH."

	1985	1986	1987	1988	1989	1990 Preliminary
Growth and inflation (*percentage change*)						
Real GDP	3.5	4.9	9.5	13.2	12.0	10.0
Real domestic demand	1.1	1.4	9.1	14.0	10.4	13.3
GDP deflator	0.7	2.9	4.5	6.2	5.2	6.8
Investment and savings (*percent of GDP*)						
Gross domestic investment[1]	24.0	21.8	23.9	28.8	31.5	37.8
Gross national savings	19.4	20.9	23.7	28.6	30.2	31.4
Statistical discrepancy	−0.6	−1.5	0.3	2.5	2.3	2.2
Foreign savings	4.0	−0.6	0.6	2.7	3.6	8.6
Unemployment rate (*percent*)	. . .	5.6	5.9	4.3	3.6	3.8
Terms of trade (*percentage change*)	−5.6	10.7	−1.0	−1.8	−3.9	−2.0
Consolidated central government (*percent of GDP, fiscal-year basis*)[2]						
Revenue and grants	16.4	16.0	16.5	17.6	18.7	20.1
Expenditure and net lending	21.7	20.8	18.7	16.9	15.3	15.3
Overall surplus or deficit	−5.4	−4.8	−2.2	0.7	3.3	4.8
Foreign borrowing (net)	1.8	1.1	0.3	0.6	−0.2	−1.6
Domestic financing (net)	3.6	3.7	1.9	−1.3	3.1	−3.2
Public sector surplus or deficit (*percent of GDP, fiscal-year basis*)[2]	−6.0	−4.8	−1.6	1.2	4.3	4.8
Money and credit (*end of year, percentage change*)						
Total domestic credit	8.4	6.1	17.6	15.6	19.8	26.9
Private credit	10.5	4.9	22.6	26.4	29.5	33.0
Total liquidity (M2)	10.3	13.4	20.2	18.2	26.3	26.7
Balance of payments (*billions of U.S. dollars*)						
Exports (f.o.b.)	7.1	8.8	11.6	15.9	19.9	22.9
Imports (c.i.f.)	−9.3	−9.3	−13.2	−19.8	−25.3	−32.7
Current account	−1.5	0.3	−0.3	−1.6	−2.4	−6.9
(*percent of GDP*)	(−4.0)	(0.7)	(−0.7)	(−2.8)	(−3.6)	(−8.6)
Overall balance (*billions of U.S. dollars*)	0.5	1.3	0.7	1.6	4.3	2.2
Reserves (*end of year, billions of U.S. dollars*)						
Gross official reserves	3.0	3.8	5.2	7.1	10.5	14.3
(*in months of imports of goods and services*)	3.9	4.8	4.7	4.3	5.0	5.3
External debt (*end of year, billions of U.S. dollars*)	17.4	18.2	19.9	20.9	22.7	29.2
(*percent of GDP*)	46.5	43.6	40.8	35.1	32.9	35.8
Debt service (*percent of exports of goods and services*)	27.5	24.8	19.8	14.9	13.0	10.9
Exchange rate						
Exchange rate (*baht/U.S. dollar, end of year*)	26.7	26.1	25.1	25.2	25.7	25.3
Real effective exchange rate[3]	89.9	84.3	77.1	76.1	80.0	78.8

Source: Data provided by the Thai authorities.
[1] Including stockbuilding.
[2] Fiscal year ended September 30.
[3] International Monetary Fund, Information Notice System index (1980 = 100).

II Overview of Economic Developments Since 1950

At the end of World War II, Thailand was a basically agrarian economy. Heavily dependent on rice, which accounted for some 25 percent of GDP, and about one half of total exports, it had only a very small manufacturing sector and limited basic infrastructure. (Box 1 presents a profile of Thailand. Box 2 describes the first 100 years of Thailand's modern economic history.) Over the ensuing 40 years, Thailand has achieved an impressive record of growth and development. Real GDP growth has averaged nearly 7 percent (Chart 1); poverty has been dramatically reduced; and output and exports have become increasingly diversified. By the end of the 1980s, Thailand was well advanced in its transition from an agricultural to an industrial and services-based economy, and is on the verge of joining the ranks of Asia's newly industrializing economies (NIEs).

Thailand's postwar development can be broadly divided into three phases. The first (1950–72) was characterized by rapid growth and development, driven from the late 1950s by the adoption of an industrial strategy that was oriented to the private sector and by a rapid improvement in infrastructure. The second (1973–85) was dominated by the need for domestic adjustment in the face of severe external shocks: attempts to maintain growth through expansionary policies in the late 1970s were followed by a series of adjustment programs designed to restore internal and external balance. From 1986 onward, these adjustment efforts, aided by a favorable external environment, began to bear fruit, and Thailand embarked on a remarkable economic expansion.

Chart 1. Selected Economic Indicators, 1953–90

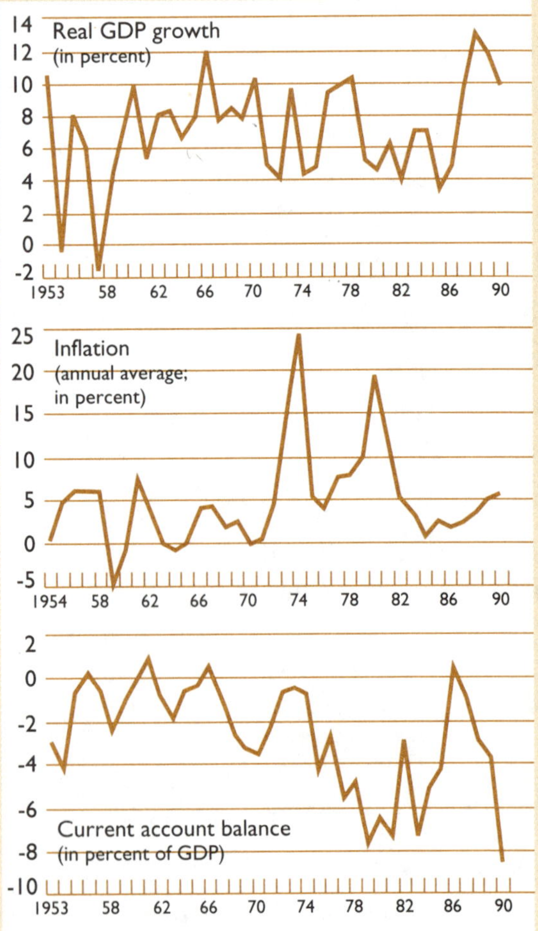

Source: Data provided by the Thai authorities.

A Market-Based Industrial Strategy, 1950–72

During the first two decades of its postwar history, Thailand's economic development was generally very successful. GDP growth averaged 5.2 percent in the 1950s, and, with the adoption of a comprehensive industrialization strategy at the turn of the decade, accelerated to an average 7.4 percent during 1960–72. Thus, despite rapid population growth, real GDP per capita doubled over the period, and the proportion of the population below the poverty line fell dramatically (Box 3). At the same time, inflation remained low, and—at least until the latter part of the 1960s—the current account deficit remained at a moderate level.

The focus of the authorities' development strategy during this period was to build up the manufacturing

Box 2. A Historical Retrospective

As of the early 1850s, Thailand was an independent and self-sufficient kingdom with a population of about 5 million. (Until 1939, it was known as Siam, but for simplicity Thailand is used throughout.) The economy, which was essentially agrarian, operated almost entirely on a subsistence basis: farmers and their families "worked just hard enough to supply themselves with the necessities of life, and custom, habit and climate kept their requirements at a modest level" (Ingram (1971), p. 19). Internal trade was mostly local, and carried out through barter, whereas, as Thailand had been virtually closed to the outside world since the seventeenth century, trade with the outside world was both extremely limited and strictly controlled.

Thailand's modern economic history really began with the accession of King Mongkut to the throne in 1851. In 1855, Thailand and Great Britain signed the Bowring Treaty, under which Thailand agreed to allow free trade in almost all products, including silver and gold; to keep tariffs at or below 3 percent; and to limit export duties. For Thailand, the treaty involved a substantial surrender of sovereignty, particularly in fiscal policy. In contrast to similar treaties imposed on China and Japan at about the same time, it seems to have been signed voluntarily, in part to head off the implicit threat of British colonial rule, but also owing to the king's conviction that Thailand's future economic development depended on its relations with the West (see Ingram (1971), p. 33).

The Bowring Treaty, which was quickly followed by similar treaties with the other major industrial powers of the time, turned Thailand practically overnight into an almost completely open economy. Buoyant foreign demand for rice, especially following the opening of the Suez Canal in 1869, combined with the free availability of cheap imported goods, prompted Thai farmers to shift from subsistence farming to production of rice as a cash crop; correspondingly, agricultural output increased, and the use of money increased dramatically. Rice exports increased some twenty-five fold between 1850 and the 1930s, to comprise about 30 percent of world trade in rice. At the same time, what was to become a long tradition of cautious financial policies began. The government budget was managed very conservatively, with only very limited recourse to foreign borrowing to finance infrastructural projects, while monetary policy was constrained both by the fixed value of the baht (first to silver and then to gold) and by the open capital account mandated by the Bowring Treaty.

Two main trends characterized Thailand's economic development during this period. First, it was based almost exclusively on increased agricultural production, particularly of rice, while the manufacturing sector remained almost completely undeveloped. Until 1919, domestic manufacturing (apart from rice and lumber milling) was almost nonexistent, and while some limited growth in manufacturing occurred in the 1930s—for instance, production of cigarettes and matches—even by 1950 the manufacturing industry accounted for less than 10 percent of GDP. Second, Thailand's development relied almost entirely on the greater use of inputs, and only slightly on growth of productivity. The technology used in rice production hardly changed over the period, and the growth in agricultural output entirely reflected the expansion of the area planted.

These trends had several, common, causes. First, since land was both abundant and freely available to anyone who would clear and cultivate it, Thailand's comparative advantage lay in land-intensive rather than in labor- or capital-intensive production. Second, until the renegotiation of the Bowring Treaty in the 1920s, manufacturing not only faced strong foreign competition as a result of low tariffs, but was further hampered by a variety of taxes (on inland transport, for instance) that the Government was unable to abolish, partly because of the constraints imposed under the Bowring Treaty on its ability to raise revenue. Third, infrastructural development—except for the railway system—was quite limited. Irrigation projects, which could have considerably improved agricultural yields, were repeatedly postponed; electricity generation capacity was very limited; and the road system was underdeveloped. Finally, although the economy became increasingly monetized, financial and capital markets were almost nonexistent. While the relative abundance of land would remain a structural feature of the Thai economy until the 1970s, the authorities moved swiftly to address the remaining problems as they sought to accelerate Thailand's industrialization in the postwar period.

sector. At the same time, investments in irrigation and the transport network contributed to high rates of growth in agricultural output and exports. After a brief—and generally unsuccessful—flirtation with state enterprises in the early 1950s,[1] from 1959 the authorities adopted an industrial strategy based on the private sector. The Board of Investment (BOI) was created to administer a package of investment incentives designed initially to promote import-substituting industries,[2] while the role of the public sector was limited to providing basic infrastructure. This strategy was in turn supported by conservative financial policies. The government deficit

[1] The Government established enterprises in a number of sectors, including textiles, paper, glass, and sugar. They proved to be generally inefficient, and since that time the role of state enterprises in the manufacturing sector has been quite limited.

[2] These included guarantees against nationalization and competition from state enterprises; tariff and business tax exemptions on imports of capital goods and raw materials; a two-year corporate tax holiday; and the possibility of import surcharges on competing imports.

Box 3. Poverty and Income Distribution

Poverty is primarily a rural phenomenon (see Table 3). About three fourths of the poor are farmers, typically located in less accessible areas, and cultivating the less profitable crops such as rainfed glutinous rice, kenaf, and jute. Correspondingly, poverty is most prevalent in the Northeast (37 percent below the poverty line), and the North (23 percent), areas characterized by relatively poor soil, low and unreliable rainfall, and poor infrastructure. (The poverty line is defined as the annual per capita household income needed to satisfy basic needs. In 1988/89, the poverty line stood at B 4,141 in rural areas and B 6,324 in urban areas.) Poverty is least important in the Bangkok Metropolitan Region (3 percent below the poverty line) in which much of Thailand's recent growth has been concentrated. But even though urban poverty is less widespread, it is relatively severe, with average family income for those in poverty in urban areas averaging 28 percent below the poverty line.

The alleviation of poverty has been a long-standing objective of the Thai authorities. Between the early 1960s and 1980, considerable progress was achieved, as rapid growth of agricultural output and incomes was supported by several specific policy programs to improve the lot of the rural poor, and the proportion of the population below the poverty line fell from close to 60 percent to some 23 percent (Table 3). In the first half of the 1980s, largely owing to declining crop prices, the proportion increased; but with the economic boom of the late 1980s, this has been largely reversed, and in 1988, the proportion of those below the poverty line had returned to its 1980 level.

But while poverty has been reduced, at least until the mid-1980s income distribution tended to become more disproportionate. The share of the top 20 percent of the population in total income increased from 49 percent in 1975 to 56 percent in 1985, while the Gini coefficient increased from 0.43 to 0.5. Perhaps unsurprisingly, the urban population, particularly in Bangkok, has received the largest share of the fruits of Thailand's economic development: between 1975 and 1985, average incomes in Bangkok increased faster than in any other region. With the economic boom in the late 1980s, there are some signs that this trend had slowed. By 1988, the share of the top 20 percent in total income had fallen to 55 percent, while the Gini coefficient declined to 0.48.

In the Seventh National Economic and Social Development Plan (1992–96), a series of measures to reduce poverty and income inequality have been proposed. In particular, concerted efforts are to be made to raise rural incomes through improvements in production, marketing and price support programs, and a greater dissemination of industrial activities into rural areas. Policies to raise income and wages, and development of human resources through better access to education and public health are to be emphasized. Also, tax policy—for instance, land, property, and inheritance taxes—will be used to reduce income disparities, while budgetary expenditures will be increasingly directed to develop health and education in rural areas. In addition to these discretionary measures, rapid economic growth and the expansion of labor-intensive manufacturing should also contribute to reducing poverty and income inequality.

Note: The above draws heavily on Hutaserani (1990) and Meesook (1979 and 1988).

Table 3. Poverty and Income Distribution, 1975–88

	1975/76	1980/81	1985/86	1988/89
Poverty incidence[1]				
Overall[1]	30	23	30	24
Urban[1]	13	8	6	7
Rural	36	27	36	29
Income distribution				
Top 10 percent	33	35	39	38
Top 20 percent	49	51	56	55
Bottom 20 percent	6	5	5	5
Gini coefficient	0.43	0.45	0.50	0.48

Source: Hutaserani (1990).
[1]Measured as the percentage of households below the poverty line.

averaged below 2 percent of GDP over the period, while monetary growth was limited to 10–15 percent annually. From 1963 onward, the exchange rate was formally linked to the U.S. dollar, to which it remained fixed—albeit with some changes in the par value—until the mid-1980s. In the tradition of Thailand's prewar development the economy continued to be very open, with current account transactions generally free, and capital controls essentially limited to outflows: at the same time, despite an increase in tariff protection, trade accounted for an increasing share of GDP.

As a result of these policies, investment soared during the 1960s, financed primarily by increasing domestic savings (Chart 2). Industrial output grew rapidly, initially in agroindustries (such as food processing) and in textiles, and then in heavy industries such as petroleum refining, chemicals, and transport equipment. Consequently, although agriculture remained the mainstay of the economy, its share in GDP fell sharply, and the dominance of rice and other traditional crops began to be challenged by new export crops (such as sugarcane, maize, and cassava) (Chart 3). This development was greatly facilitated by substantial improvements in the infrastructure, notably in irrigation, electricity supply, and transportation, and by the growth of the commercial banking system, particularly during the 1950s. The improvement of the road system opened up the domestic market for Thailand's nascent

Chart 2. Investment and Savings, 1950–90
(As percent of GDP)

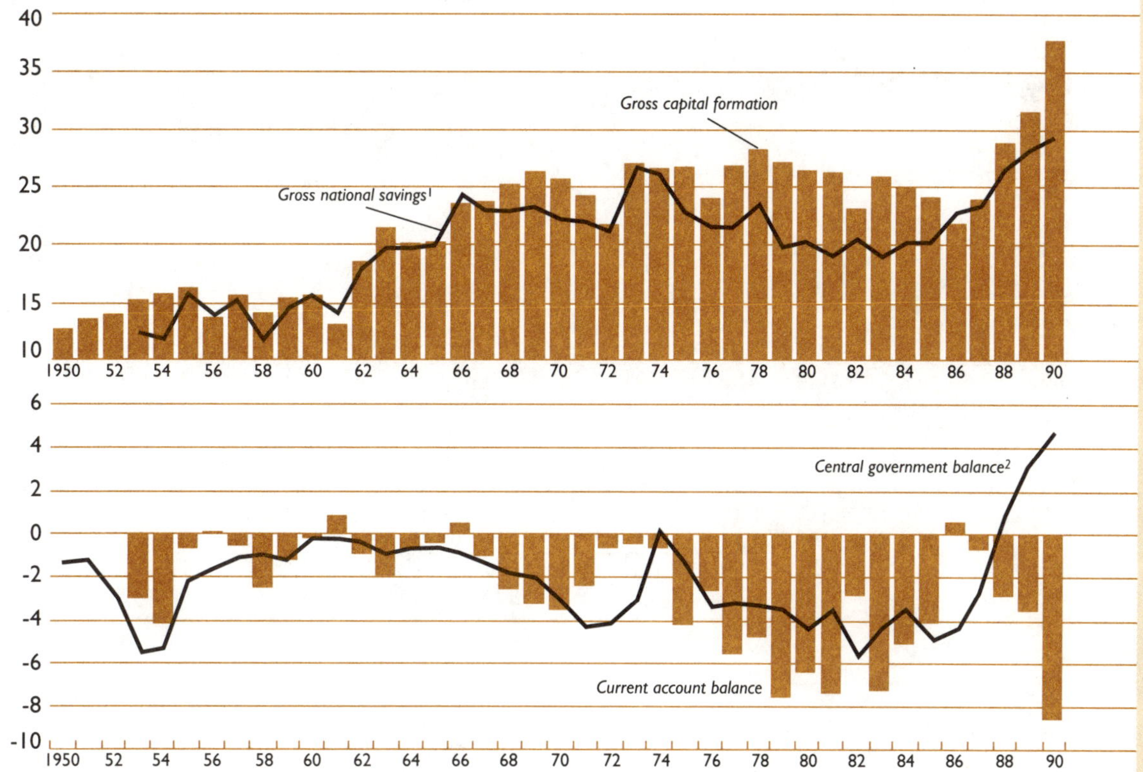

Source: Data provided by the Thai authorities.
[1]Derived as gross capital formation plus the current account balance.
[2]On a fiscal-year basis.

manufacturing industry, while allowing agricultural production in the provinces to be sent to Bangkok for export.[3]

Toward the end of the 1960s, however, it became clear that, given Thailand's small domestic market, the limits of efficient import substitution would be quickly reached. At the same time, the industrialization strategy had contributed to a structural deterioration in the trade balance (Chart 4): manufacturing exports remained small, export diversification was limited to nontraditional agricultural products, whereas imports of raw materials and capital goods by import-substituting industries had grown rapidly. Although the impact on the current account was partly offset by a boom in service receipts associated with the Vietnam war, balance of payments deficits emerged in 1969 and 1970. From 1969 onward, there was a conscious shift in policies away from import substitution toward export promotion: in 1972 the investment incentive law was amended to give greater incentives to export industries. Thus, despite a tariff regime that continued to favor import-competing production, the growth of the manufacturing sector from this time on became increasingly export oriented.

External Shocks and Domestic Adjustment, 1973–85

The period 1973–85, during which Thailand faced a cumulative deterioration in its terms of trade of about 36 percent, was perhaps the most difficult in economic

[3] As one example of this, the improvement of transportation links with the Northeast led to a substantial increase in exports of cassava.

Chart 3. External Developments, 1953–90

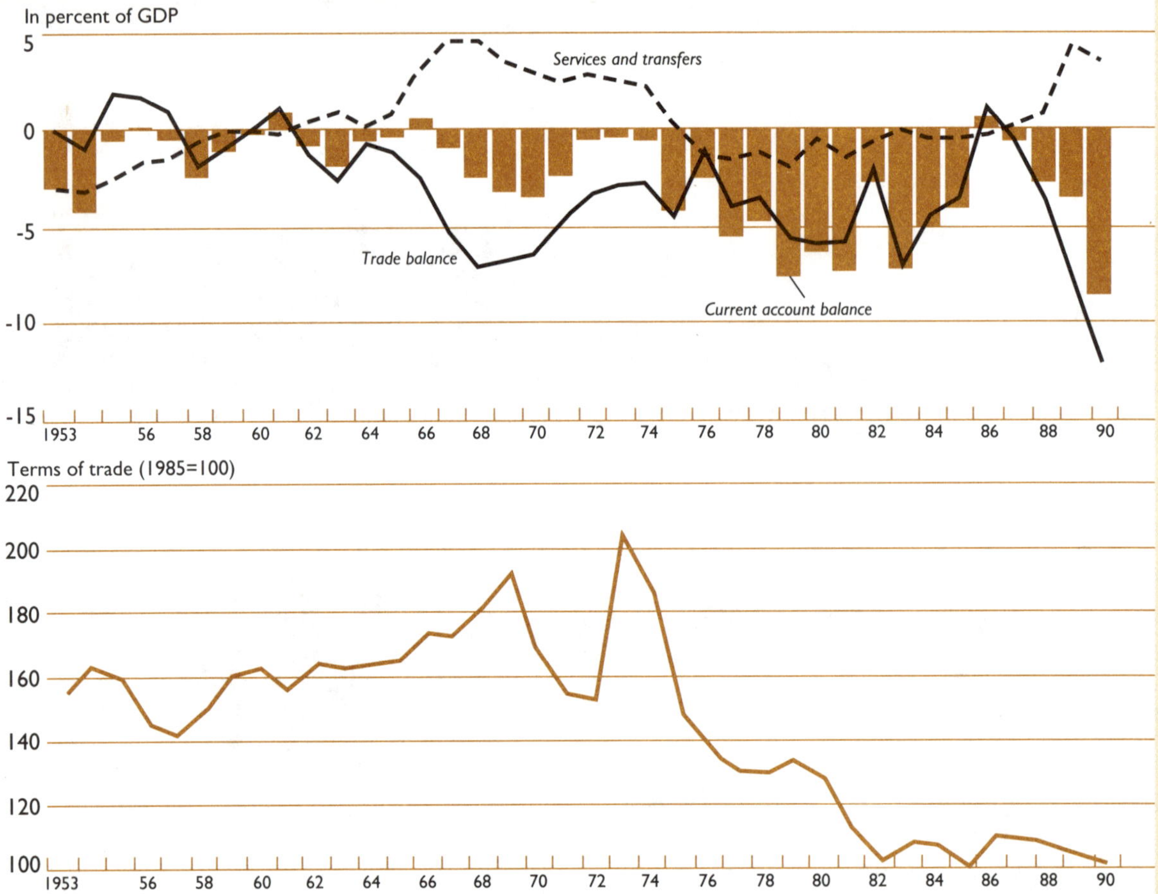

Source: Data provided by the Thai authorities.

terms in Thailand's postwar history. Real GDP growth in most years was well below the levels of the previous period; inflation rose sharply in the period immediately after the two oil shocks; and a substantial and persistent current account deficit emerged, which led to a significant increase in Thailand's external debt and debt service. Even so, largely because the authorities adopted adjustment policies before these problems became acute, Thailand's difficulties were moderate compared with those of many other developing countries, and it enjoyed access to international capital markets throughout the period.

While adjustment to the external shocks was initially delayed, the authorities changed policies pragmatically as macroeconomic and structural imbalances became increasingly evident. Following the first oil shock, the primary concern of policymakers was to restore past rates of economic growth. To this end, public expenditures were increased sharply, with particularly rapid growth in infrastructural investment and outlays on defense; and a substantial fiscal deficit emerged, financed increasingly through foreign borrowing. Prices of certain key inputs, including oil, were maintained at well below world market levels; and tariffs and other trade barriers designed to protect domestic industries were increased markedly.

While this strategy resulted in a pickup in growth, its limitations were rapidly exposed by the second oil shock in 1979. Despite buoyant export growth—owing in part to the incentives adopted earlier in the decade—the trade balance deteriorated sharply, and the impact on the current account was exacerbated by a decline in services receipts caused by the closure of U.S. bases in Thailand at the end of the Vietnam war. While there

Chart 4. Indicators of Structural Change, 1950–90

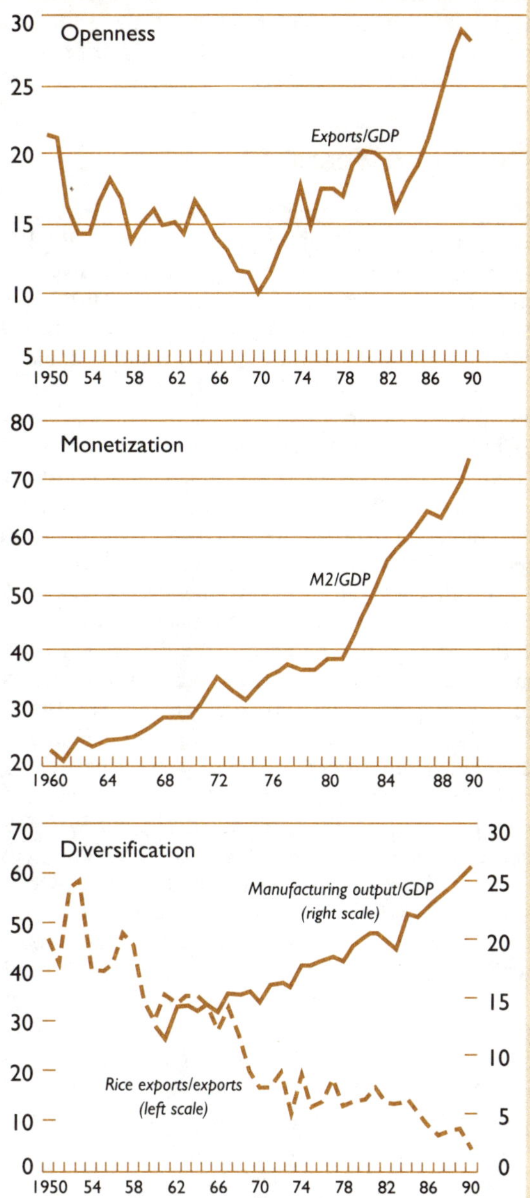

Source: Data provided by the Thai authorities.

was no immediate difficulty in financing the deficit, and the stock of foreign debt and level of debt service remained moderate by international standards, the rapid rate of accumulation of debt became an increasing concern. At the same time, the structure of domestic prices had become increasingly skewed, as the effects of the price controls and higher tariff protection were compounded by a steady appreciation of the real exchange rate and the emergence of negative real interest rates. This not only led to resource misallocation, but also directly contributed to the domestic imbalances. For example, subsidized energy prices not only affected the fiscal position but also—because they had discouraged energy conservation—exacerbated the impact of higher foreign oil prices on the external accounts. It became clear therefore that, without a change in policies, the deterioration in the external payments situation and distortions in relative prices would be unsustainable and would undermine the economy's growth potential over the long term. In recognition of this, from 1980 onward, the authorities embarked on a comprehensive adjustment program, supported by three stand-by arrangements with the IMF (together with drawings under the compensatory financing facility and the buffer stock facility) and two structural adjustment loans from the World Bank.[4] Key objectives of this program, set out in the Fifth National Economic and Social Development Plan, included the reduction of the twin fiscal and current account deficits, the elimination of distortions in relative prices, and a reversal of the protectionist trend of the late 1970s.

During the following five years, although a variety of expenditure and revenue measures were implemented, little sustained progress was made in strengthening the fiscal position, and the current account deficit remained consistently high. While this reflected a number of factors, including the difficulties caused by a further deterioration of the terms of trade in 1981–82, there were two key underlying problems: a chronic tendency to overestimate revenues that meant—given the innate difficulty of reducing expenditures in midyear—that the deficit was consistently higher than budgeted; and the inelasticity of the tax system, owing mainly to a plethora of tax exemptions. Yet while the macroeconomic imbalances persisted, considerable progress was made in other areas. Domestic prices of energy products were raised to world levels, eliminating the disincentive to energy conservation that had contributed to the current account deficits of the late 1970s. Controls on domestic interest rates were relaxed, and interest rate ceilings increased. This, together with progress in reducing inflation, contributed to steadily positive real interest rates from 1982 onward (Chart 5) and to rapid increases in the monetization of the economy and in the growth of the domestic banking system. Export

[4] The three Fund stand-by arrangements were for SDR 814.5 million, approved in June 1981; for SDR 271.5 million approved in November 1982; and for SDR 400 million, approved in May 1985. In July 1981, drawings under the compensatory financing facility, for SDR 186 million, and the buffer stock financing facility, for SDR 17 million, were also approved. The World Bank's first structural adjustment loan, for $150 million, was approved in May 1982, followed by a second, for $175.5 million, in March 1983.

Chart 5. Interest Rates and Exchange Rates, 1978–90

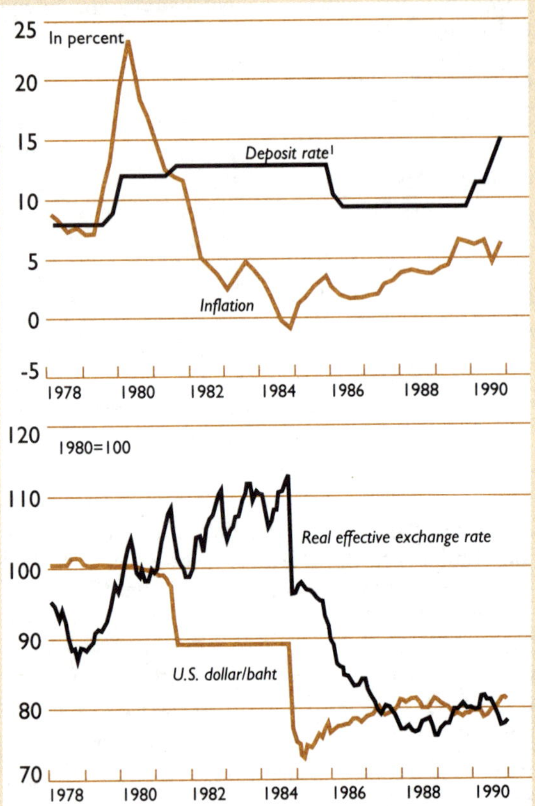

Source: Data provided by the Thai authorities.
[1]Maximum rate on 3-6 month deposit at commercial banks.

taxes and quantitative restrictions on imports were also reduced, and the dispersion in tariff rates was narrowed, but—partly because of the fiscal situation—little sustained progress was made in reducing the level of import tariffs (see Section V). Finally, the external competitiveness of the Thai economy—which had been further eroded as the baht appreciated with the U.S. dollar during the early 1980s—was strengthened through a 14.8 percent devaluation against the U.S. dollar in November 1984.[5]

A far-reaching development that occurred during these years was a slowdown in the rate of growth of cultivated land, as the limits of Thailand's land frontier began to be reached. Thus, Thailand's relative abundance of land, which had been a dominating influence on the pattern of development over the past 120 years (Box 1), began to fade, reinforcing the shift toward labor-intensive manufacturing that was already under way.

The Boom Years, 1986–90

Since 1986, Thailand has experienced an economic boom, unparalleled in its postwar history. Real GDP has risen by an average of over 11 percent a year, high both in absolute terms and in comparison with other dynamic countries in the region. Manufacturing output and exports have not only increased but become more diversified: more than half of the export growth over the period has been due to nontraditional exports, including computer parts, consumer electronics, travel goods, and toys. At the same time, both construction—associated with a boom in real estate prices and development—and services, particularly in the financial sector and in tourism, have grown rapidly.

The driving forces underlying the expansion have been twofold: first, a boom in manufacturing exports, which have grown by an average 29 percent annually in volume terms during the period; and second, a surge in private investment, particularly in the export-oriented manufacturing sector, whose share in GDP more than doubled, from 14 percent to 29 percent between 1986 and 1990. These developments, in turn, had several common causes. First, as noted above, by 1986 the depreciation of the baht had improved the competitiveness of Thai exports. Second, particularly after 1988, Thailand—like other countries in the region—benefited from a surge in foreign direct investment, much of which reflected plant relocations from Japan and the Asian NIEs in response to economic restructuring in those countries. Third, export growth was also boosted by the elimination of most export taxes and other burdens on exporters, while domestic costs—particularly wages—remained quite low relative to Thailand's main competitors.

The sustainability of the boom was greatly enhanced by a sharp improvement in the fiscal position; thus, despite a decline in private savings, the current account deficit remained—until 1990—well below the levels of the previous decade. The public sector deficit of 5 percent of GDP in 1984/85 was eliminated by 1987/88, and by 1989/90 the public sector was running a surplus of close to 5 percent of GDP, a swing of 10 percent of GDP. The reasons for this dramatic success, which had eluded policymakers for so long, are analyzed in more detail in Section III. But the most important factor was a reversal of the previous practice of revenue overestimation toward an even more pro-

[5] In November 1984, the link of the Thai baht to the U.S. dollar was formally abandoned, and the value of the baht is now determined in relation to a basket of currencies reflecting the composition of Thailand's trade and settlements. In practice, however, the baht has continued to move quite closely with the dollar: thus, just as it appreciated with the dollar in the early 1980s, it also followed the dollar downward in 1985 and 1986.

nounced tendency toward revenue underestimation, thus imparting into the system an institutional bias toward fiscal surpluses that was in practice compounded by higher-than-expected GNP growth.

By late 1989, however, it had become clear that the strength of Thailand's economy had brought with it a number of problems. Infrastructural bottlenecks—which had been apparent for a number of years—became increasingly serious, especially in transportation, port capacity, and water and electricity supply (see Box 5 in Section III for a summary of these problems). At the same time, shortages of skilled labor, particularly engineers and technicians, began to emerge. Moreover, the strength of investment demand was reflected in buoyant capital inflows and in increasing balance of payments surpluses, resulting in turn in accelerated monetary growth, which the Bank of Thailand found increasingly difficult to sterilize, given the openness of the capital account and the limited monetary instruments at its disposal.[6] As one symptom of these developments, the current account deteriorated, while inflation—although not far out of line with trading partners—edged upward, and asset prices, particularly of real estate and stocks, surged, thereby causing growing concern that the economy might be overheating.

In response, the authorities implemented a series of measures in early 1990 to reduce excess liquidity and dampen credit demand, including the reintroduction of a 10 percent withholding tax on interest payments on foreign loans; the abolition of ceilings on deposit interest rates; an increase in the lending rate ceiling from 15 percent to 16.5 percent; and the sale of B 13.5 billion of Bank of Thailand bonds (equivalent to about 8 percent of reserve money). These measures were backed up by the introduction of voluntary limits on commercial bank lending to "nonproductive" activities, including purchases of consumer durables and real estate and construction of luxury condominiums and golf courses. At the same time, although public investment in infrastructure was boosted, fiscal policy remained tight, with buoyant revenues raising the overall public sector surplus in 1989/90 to 4.8 percent of GDP, the highest level on record.

These measures, combined with the impact of the Middle East crisis from early August, did result in some slowdown in demand pressures toward the end of the year, which was reinforced by a further tightening of monetary policy in November when the lending rate ceiling was raised further to 19 percent. Nevertheless, for the year as a whole, demand growth remained very strong, led by a further sharp increase in investment. As a result—and reflecting also the temporary impact of a drought-induced reduction in agricultural exports and higher oil prices in the second half of the year—the current account deficit increased sharply, to about 8.6 percent of GDP, the highest level since the late seventies. Even so, the balance of payments remained in strong surplus, owing largely to a substantial increase in private nonbank borrowing.

[6] A discussion of the effect of capital mobility on monetary policy in Thailand can be found in Appendix I.

Policy Challenges for the 1990s

The main economic challenge for Thai policymakers continues to be how best to sustain the expansion of the past four years, while at the same time avoiding overheating the economy and beginning to eliminate infrastructural and other constraints to growth in the longer term. In the short term, while inflation appears on a downward trend, the current account deficit increased sharply in 1990. This increase is, to a considerable extent, the natural consequence of Thailand's rapid industrialization. In marked contrast to earlier periods, the deficit has not been due to higher public sector deficits (indeed the public sector is in historically high surplus) but to booming private sector investment, much of which has been concentrated in export-oriented industry; moreover, it is more than financed by capital inflows. Even so, if the deficit were to continue at present levels over a longer period, external debt and debt service would grow considerably, and Thailand's vulnerability to external shocks would be correspondingly increased. Consequently, the authorities intend to continue to implement cautious fiscal and monetary policies, combined with measures to encourage both exports and private savings, so as to facilitate a steady reduction in the deficit over the medium term.

In the long term, however, the most crucial issues are structural in nature. As noted above, strains on the domestic infrastructure and in certain segments of the labor markets have become increasingly apparent in recent years. While the impact on growth may so far have been slight—it is believed, for example, that the return on foreign investment in Thailand remains very competitive with that in neighboring countries—it is unlikely to remain so indefinitely unless corrective action is taken. Moreover, these strains have added to inflationary pressures, and in some cases have brought both environmental and health problems in their wake (see Box 4 for an overview of environmental problems in Thailand). Public investment in infrastructure has been increased, and—as described in more detail in Section III—a wide-ranging program of infrastructural projects is now under consideration, in which the private sector is expected to play a leading role. While the timing and status of many of these projects have yet to be determined, they will likely require substantial investment, which in turn reinforces the need to strengthen domestic savings if excessive recourse to foreign borrowing is to be avoided. To support this,

Box 4. Environmental Issues

One undesirable side effect of Thailand's rapid growth has been an increase in environmental problems. Economic development has damaged the environment by encroaching on natural areas and threatening existing ecosystems. At the same time, rapid industrialization, migration, and population growth have put increasing pressures on urban areas, straining existing infrastructure and resources, exacerbating urban congestion, and contributing to noise, air, and water pollution.

In response to these problems, government programs since the early 1980s have begun to focus on the need to balance economic growth with environmental improvement. Standards for national air quality were introduced in early 1981, and for noise pollution from land and water vehicles in 1985. A master plan for rural water supply and sanitation was also completed in 1985; the use of environmental impact assessments in the design of major projects was increased; and a variety of sector-specific measures were taken.

At present, the main areas of concern include

- Air and noise pollution, particularly in the Bangkok area, which is caused mainly by traffic (including long-tailed boats) and industry, and much of which is not equipped with pollution control equipment. Concentrations of suspended particulates and carbon monoxide in Bangkok reportedly exceed standards set by Thailand's National Environment Board (NEB), although concentrations of ambient lead have dropped, owing to the reduction in 1984 in the lead limit for gasoline, and also to the greater use of diesel oil and liquefied petroleum gas.
- Water conservation is crucial in the Bangkok area, where increased private underground water extraction from artesian wells in response to the unreliable public water supply has resulted in subsidence and frequent flooding. The lack of waste treatment facilities poses an additional threat to water supplies through contamination of both surface water and groundwater, while the dumping of solid wastes from factories and the drainage of agricultural wastes contribute to cumulative pollution problems, especially in the lower sectors of the Chao Phraya and Tha Chin Rivers feeding into the upper part of the Gulf of Thailand. In response to these problems, the authorities plan to increase the capacity of the Bang Khen water treatment plant by over 50 percent by 1994, and to boost the supply of untreated water to the plant through a canal to the Tha Chin—and ultimately the Mae Klong—Rivers by the year 2000, which should eliminate the need for artesian wells. To combat industrial pollution, the NEB has laid down similar standards on industrial location and water production by factories, although enforcement of these rules is complicated by the large number of plants operating in the Bangkok area.
- Land and soils have been eroded through deforestation, until recently at an annual rate of 1.5 percent. The disappearance of many rain forests in Southern Thailand was a major factor in the disastrous floods of October 1988, which prompted the Government to impose a nationwide ban on logging. In addition, the Government has set a minimum target for forest coverage of 40 percent of Thailand's total land area (compared with the current level of 29 percent), although at the current rate of replanting this would take over a century to achieve. The expansion of agriculture into watersheds and marginal areas, the runoff from agricultural enterprises, and the expansion of freshwater shrimp farming have also led to environmental problems.
- Fisheries in both the Gulf of Thailand and the Andaman Sea have been depleted through modern fishing techniques. In response, the authorities capped the number of trawlers in 1983, and more recently banned fishing within three miles of the shoreline. Freshwater catches are also declining because of overexploitation.
- Thailand's coastal zone consists largely of mangrove forests, which serve as important habitats for many species of marine life and are a vital part of marine ecosystems. These have, however, been depleted for charcoal production or cleared for industrial or residential development. Management areas are being established to control mangrove exploitation and promote reforestation, while more generally the Government is implementing a project to develop and manage the coastal zones.

The Seventh National Economic and Social Development Plan (1992–96) reiterates the need to promote the effective use of natural resources and to conserve the environment. To this end, a tripartite effort, by the Government, the business sector, and the public, is envisaged to protect, maintain, and monitor the environment; and plans for infrastructure will include an assessment of the environmental impact and measures to limit any resulting adverse effects. Priority will be given to addressing the problems of air pollution (through controls on emissions of sulfur dioxide and other gases, and restrictions on the lead content of fuel oil); acid rain (through better combustion technologies and the installation of pollution control devices); and water quality and the disposal of solid waste (through restrictions on the sites of new factories and investment in new waste water treatment facilities). Taxes or fines on enterprises that damage the environment or fail to install pollution control equipment are also envisaged.

the authorities have also taken a number of steps to reduce shortages of skilled labor, including guidelines to encourage training for apprentices and those wishing to upgrade their skills, and measures to increase the output of engineering and technical graduates. The draft Seventh National Economic and Social Development Plan also envisages an increase in the minimum period of schooling from six to nine years.

A second important issue for Thailand as it makes the transition from an agricultural to an industrial and services-based economy is the deregulation of domestic markets. In this area, compared with many other developing countries, Thailand is already well advanced: the public enterprise sector has historically been relatively small and efficient; while some price controls exist, domestic prices are largely market determined, and the current and capital accounts of the balance of payments have historically been very open.[7] The main focuses of regulatory reform are the financial system (particularly the development of the capital market); the tax system, including the replacement of the business tax by a value-added tax (VAT); and the trade system, where the distortions caused by high nominal tariffs and effective rates of protection are likely to pose an increasingly important obstacle to both output and export growth (see Section V).

Finally, efforts to improve the quality of economic growth, which has been affected in recent years by both environmental problems and by a deterioration in income distribution, will be crucial to ensure the substainability of Thailand's development over the longer term. As, on the one hand, the role of government recedes through deregulation and the various reforms designed to strengthen the role of the private sector, policymakers will need to devote increasing attention to the development of new, market-based instruments to reduce the environmental costs of economic development and to improve income distribution, while minimizing the impact on incentives and growth. These issues, and the reform proposals the authorities are currently proposing, are taken up in more detail in the following sections.

[7] In May 1990, Thailand accepted the obligations of Article VIII, Sections 2, 3, and 4 of the Fund's Articles of Agreement. This was followed in April 1991 by a series of measures to liberalize capital account transactions further: in particular, Thai investors were permitted to transfer freely up to $5 million abroad for domestic investment overseas, and foreign exchange earners were allowed to open foreign exchange accounts with commercial banks in Thailand. The remaining capital account restrictions relate mainly to purchases of real estate, equity, and financial instruments abroad, all of which are subject to approval by the central bank.

III Fiscal Adjustment in the 1980s and Beyond

A critical element of the adjustment policies that helped set the stage for Thailand's remarkable economic performance in the late 1980s was the sustained improvement in public sector finances.[8] Consolidated public sector deficits averaging 7 percent of GDP at the start of the decade gave way to surpluses of over 4 percent of GDP toward the end of the 1980s (Table 4). Although this turnaround was certainly facilitated by the buoyant revenue growth associated with vigorous economic expansion in the latter half of the 1980s, the shift in public sector finances was more than just cyclical and involved conservative policies plus fundamental changes in expenditure control and in the budgetary process.

Overview of Adjustment Effort

As part of their broader strategy to narrow external current account imbalances, the Thai authorities made a number of attempts in the early 1980s to reduce the size of the public sector deficit. Although many revenue measures were taken,[9] these efforts focused mainly on the expenditure side. The principal elements of expenditure reduction included a conservative wage policy (government pay scales were not substantively revised between 1982 and 1989, and cost of living allowances were targeted to the lowest-paid workers); a reduction in capital expenditures in successive budgets totaling about 1 percent of GDP; and price increases and lower investment by public enterprises that reduced their financing requirements by over 2 percent of GDP between 1980/81 and 1984/85.[10] Although these efforts were partly offset by rising interest payments on public debt, they were of critical importance insofar as they set the tone for expenditure policy for the remainder of the decade.

However, these policies proved inadequate for the immediate task of reducing the fiscal deficit during the early 1980s. Thwarting deficit reduction was a fundamental weakness in the budgetary process: a chronic tendency to overestimate revenues (by an average of 1.5 percent of GDP), when combined with the lack of flexibility in scaling back expenditures once they had been budgeted, meant that the overall deficit was persistently larger than targeted. Recognition of this problem brought about a major shift in the budgetary process starting with the 1986/87 budget. Since then, decidedly conservative revenue estimates (now underestimating revenues, on average, by over 2 percent of GDP) have helped check budgeted expenditure and imparted an institutional bias toward the generation of fiscal surpluses.

Total revenue and grants expanded from less than 16 percent of GDP in the first half of the decade to over 20 percent of GDP by 1989/90. The marked growth in central government revenue was entirely due to higher tax receipts, in turn a reflection of the vigorous pace of economic activity during the second half of the decade. The most significant increases were from income and corporate taxes, as well as from the business tax on gross turnover. Indeed, the growth in the underlying base of these taxes was more than sufficient to offset revenue losses that might have arisen from the downward revision in income and corporate tax rates in 1986. Revenues from import tariffs also grew strongly, particularly in the second half of the decade when booming domestic investment induced a rapidly growing volume of imports; however, these receipts were partly offset by the loss of revenues caused by eliminating most export taxes in early 1985. Even so, taken as a whole, average tax buoyancy rose sharply, from just over 1.1 during the first half of the decade to nearly 1.7 during the late 1980s. Among the factors contributing to higher revenue buoyancy was the expansion of activities covered in the tax net (for example, the shift in output from agriculture to manufacturing and the increase in imports as a share of GDP).

[8] The public sector consists of the Central Government and two specialized funds (the Farmer's Aid Fund and the Rubber Replanting Fund). A broader definition of the public sector would consolidate the accounts of local governments and some 50 nonfinancial public enterprises, including the Oil Fund. This section focuses on the narrower concept of the public sector.

[9] These included increases in a variety of taxes, notably import duties and excises; the introduction of an exit tax for residents traveling abroad; measures to increase the tax base, especially for income and corporate taxes; and efforts to improve tax administration and collection.

[10] An overall ceiling on the external debt of public enterprises also limited capital spending and increased pressure on them to improve their efficiency.

Table 4. Accounts of the Central Government, 1980/81–1989/90[1]

	1980/81	1981/82	1982/83	1983/84	1984/85	1985/86	1986/87	1987/88	1988/89	1989/90
					(In billions of baht)					
Total revenue and grants	115.5	118.8	139.4	152.2	164.3	172.1	200.1	253.8	318.5	403.3
Revenue	111.8	116.3	136.4	148.2	160.5	166.7	193.2	248.0	312.2	396.7
Tax	100.7	104.7	123.4	134.6	143.0	149.4	174.6	228.0	285.3	365.1
Nontax	11.1	11.6	13.0	13.6	17.5	17.3	18.6	20.0	26.9	31.6
Grants	3.7	2.6	3.0	3.9	3.8	5.4	6.9	5.8	6.3	6.6
Total expenditure and net lending	140.9	167.8	177.4	189.3	218.3	223.3	227.2	243.4	261.4	306.7
Current expenditure	110.2	126.7	140.5	155.9	171.4	178.5	185.3	196.9	220.6	246.4
Capital expenditure	32.3	38.4	36.0	34.4	41.6	40.1	37.2	35.9	38.6	55.9
Net lending	−1.6	2.9	0.8	−1.0	5.3	4.7	4.7	10.6	2.2	4.4
Overall balance	−25.4	−49.0	−38.0	−37.2	−54.0	−51.2	−27.1	10.4	57.1	96.6
Financing	25.4	49.0	38.0	37.2	54.0	51.2	27.1	−10.4	−57.1	−96.6
External	5.6	14.2	8.2	4.8	18.1	11.4	4.0	8.3	−3.8	−32.3
Domestic	19.7	34.8	29.8	32.2	35.8	39.9	23.1	−18.7	−53.3	−64.3
Bank	16.6	29.5	13.5	21.8	2.5	15.6	7.1	−43.4	−49.3	−66.8
Other	3.2	5.3	16.3	10.5	33.4	24.2	16.0	24.7	−4.0	2.5
					(In percent of GDP)[2]					
Total revenue and grants	15.7	14.8	15.7	15.9	16.4	16.0	16.5	17.6	18.7	20.1
Revenue	15.2	14.4	15.4	15.5	16.0	15.5	15.9	17.2	18.3	19.8
Tax	13.7	13.0	13.9	14.1	14.2	13.9	14.4	15.8	16.7	18.2
Nontax	1.5	1.4	1.5	1.4	1.7	1.6	1.5	1.4	1.6	1.6
Grants	0.5	0.3	0.3	0.4	0.4	0.5	0.6	0.4	0.4	0.3
Total expenditure and net lending	19.2	20.8	20.0	19.8	21.7	20.8	18.7	16.9	15.3	15.3
Current expenditure	15.0	15.7	15.8	16.3	17.1	16.6	15.3	13.6	12.9	12.3
Capital expenditure	4.4	4.8	4.1	3.6	4.1	3.7	3.1	2.5	2.3	2.8
Net lending	−0.2	0.4	0.1	−0.1	0.5	0.4	0.4	0.7	0.1	0.2
Overall balance	−3.5	−6.1	−4.3	−3.9	−5.4	−4.8	−2.2	0.7	3.3	4.8
Financing	3.5	6.1	4.3	3.9	5.4	4.8	2.2	−0.7	−3.3	−4.8
External	0.8	1.8	1.0	0.5	1.8	1.1	0.3	0.6	−0.2	−1.6
Domestic	2.7	4.3	3.3	3.4	3.6	3.7	1.9	−1.3	−3.2	−3.2
Bank[3]	2.3	3.7	1.5	2.3	0.2	1.5	0.6	−3.0	−2.9	−3.3
Other	0.4	0.6	1.8	1.1	3.3	2.2	1.3	1.7	−0.2	0.1
Memorandum items:										
Consolidated public sector[4]	−6.9	−8.0	−6.0	−4.6	−6.0	−4.8	−1.6	1.2	4.3	4.8
Of which: All NFPEs	−3.6	−2.2	−1.6	−0.7	−1.4	−0.7	0.3	−0.4	0.6	−0.3
(NFPEs excluding Oil Fund)	−3.3	−2.1	−1.7	−1.1	−1.0	−0.7	0.3	−0.4	0.7	−0.4

Source: International Monetary Fund, *Government Finance Statistics (GFS)*.
[1]Includes the operations of the Farmer's Aid Fund and the Rubber Replanting Fund. Table is in *GFS* format.
[2]On a fiscal-year basis.
[3]As recorded in the monetary survey.
[4]Consolidates the accounts of the Central Government, local governments, and nonfinancial public enterprises (NFPEs).

The general trend in expenditure has been downward, with its ratio to GDP declining from an average of 20 percent of GDP to about 15 percent of GDP in recent years. The bulk of the adjustment has been in current expenditures, which have fallen more or less across the board (Chart 6). The largest declines were in spending on goods and services and on interest payments (the latter reflecting the reduction in government debt following the successive fiscal surpluses). Also, as noted earlier, government pay scales were not substantively revised between 1982 and 1989—which brought down the total wage bill after 1986 (though not without adverse effects on the ability of the Government to retain and recruit qualified personnel). Central government capital expenditures also fell by over 1.5 percent of GDP during the 1980s. For the most part, this was the outcome of a deliberate effort to avoid large and potentially wasteful capital projects until the need for

Chart 6. Central Government Revenue and Expenditure, 1980/81–1990/91

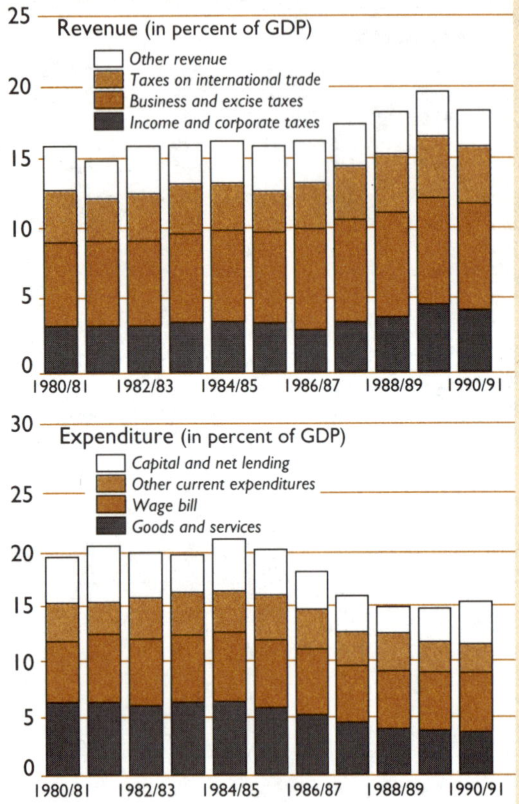

Source: Data provided by the Thai authorities.

them was clearly demonstrated. In retrospect, this conservative policy of having capital spending follow demand, rather than anticipate it, was not without its costs, particularly in the late 1980s when infrastructural bottlenecks became increasingly apparent. Despite larger budgetary outlays in response to such needs, capital spending continued to decline as an unintended by-product of capacity constraints in the booming construction sector and because of delays in approving cost increases in such an environment.

Can fiscal policy in the 1980s be characterized as essentially countercyclical in nature? Table 5 sheds some light on this question by presenting estimates of fiscal stance and impulse. The former, defined as the difference between the actual and cyclically neutral budget, quantifies the extent to which the budget added or withdrew demand relative to an equilibrium potential output level; fiscal impulse, defined as the change in the fiscal stance, measures the extent to which fiscal policy becomes more or less expansionary.[11] Table 5, which takes 1987/88 as a base year in which output is deemed to be at its potential (noninflationary) level, confirms that the fiscal stance was indeed countercyclical through most of the 1980s.[12] Of course, both discretionary policies (specifically, the expenditure restraint evident during the cyclical upswing of the late 1980s) and automatic stabilizers (for example, the responsiveness of revenues to income growth) have played a role in the countercyclical behavior of the budget.

Medium-Term Issues in Public Sector

The agenda for the public sector over the medium term is dominated by three closely related issues. First, investment in infrastructure has to be stepped up if the growth momentum is to be sustained. Second, tax reform, including the replacement of the business tax by a value-added tax, reductions in tariffs, and a realignment of income and corporate taxes, is needed to improve economic efficiency. And third, if the first two objectives work to reduce the public sector surplus, they have to be implemented in a manner that takes into account the imperatives of macroeconomic balance.

Infrastructural Bottlenecks

The rapid growth of output in recent years has placed increasing strains on Thailand's infrastructure (see Box 5). These have been particularly palpable in the Bangkok metropolitan area, the geographical heart of the economic boom. However, the phenomenon is more than just a problem of excessive strain on urban facilities, as there is some evidence that shortages of skilled labor and infrastructure (notably water and communications) may be raising production costs in other parts of the country as well. Failure to address such shortages would therefore have serious implications for the economy's cost structure and for the sustainability of its growth momentum.

In responding to these needs, the Government has sought to redefine the roles of the public and private sectors in the development of Thailand's infrastructure. The new policy, which aims at increasing private sector participation in infrastructure and services, is not geared toward privatization of existing enterprises (an approach partly circumscribed by labor union resistance). Rather, it gives a leading role to the private sector wherever major new initiatives are required. Thus, two of the largest infrastructural projects presently under consideration—a major expansion in the telephone network and

[11] See Heller, Haas, and Mansur (1986).

[12] Alternative assumptions about the base year and the level of potential output, to which estimates of fiscal stance are known to be sensitive, yield a generally similar characterization of fiscal policy.

Table 5. Estimation of Fiscal Stance and Impulse, 1980/81–1989/90

	1980/81	1981/82	1982/83	1983/84	1984/85	1985/86	1986/87	1987/88	1988/89	1989/90
					(In billions of baht)					
Neutral revenue and grants[1]	129.2	141.5	156.0	168.4	176.5	189.0	213.4	253.8	299.9	352.0
Neutral expenditure and net lending[2]	121.4	136.8	151.9	164.1	176.9	194.2	217.1	246.4	269.7	306.1
Actual expenditure and net lending	140.9	167.8	177.4	189.3	218.3	223.3	227.2	243.4	261.4	306.7
Neutral budget	7.8	4.8	4.1	4.3	−0.3	−5.2	−3.6	7.4	30.2	45.9
Actual budget	−25.4	−49.0	−38.0	−37.2	−54.0	−51.2	−27.1	10.4	57.1	96.6
Fiscal stance[3]	33.2	53.8	42.1	41.4	53.7	46.0	23.5	−2.9	−26.9	−50.7
Fiscal impulse[4]	. . .	20.6	−11.6	−0.7	12.2	−7.7	−22.5	−26.4	−24.0	−23.8
					(In percent of GDP)					
Neutral revenue and grants[1]	17.6	17.6	17.6	17.6	17.6	17.6	17.6	17.6	17.6	17.6
Actual revenue and grants	15.8	14.8	15.7	15.9	16.4	16.0	16.5	17.6	18.6	20.1
Neutral expenditure and net lending[2]	16.5	17.0	17.1	17.1	17.6	18.1	17.9	17.1	15.8	15.3
Actual expenditure and net lending	19.2	20.8	20.0	19.8	21.7	20.8	18.7	16.9	15.3	15.4
Neutral budget	1.1	0.6	0.5	0.4	—	−0.5	−0.3	0.5	1.8	2.3
Actual budget	−3.5	−6.1	−4.3	−3.9	−5.4	−4.8	−2.2	0.7	3.3	4.8
Fiscal stance[3]	4.5	6.7	4.7	4.3	5.3	4.3	1.9	−0.2	−1.6	−2.5
Fiscal impulse[4]	. . .	2.6	−1.3	−0.1	1.2	−0.7	−1.9	−1.8	−1.4	−1.2
Memorandum items:										
Nominal GDP[5] *(in baht)*	734.8	805.1	887.6	957.6	1,004.2	1,075.1	1,213.8	1,443.6	1,705.9	2,002.2
Potential GDP[5] *(in baht)*	720.0	811.1	900.8	973.0	1,048.8	1,151.9	1,287.1	1,461.0	1,599.4	1,815.2
Real growth[5] *(percent)*	5.0	4.1	7.2	7.1	3.5	4.9	9.5	13.2	12.0	10.0

Sources: Data provided by the Thai authorities; and IMF staff estimates.
[1]Base revenue ratio times actual GDP.
[2]Base expenditure ratio times potential GDP.
[3]Neutral budget minus actual budget.
[4]Change in fiscal stance.
[5]On a fiscal-year basis.

the development of a light rail system to serve the Bangkok area—are to be undertaken and financed by the private sector. The private sector is also expected to take the lead in a telecommunications satellite project and in the construction and operation of an elevated highway. In most of these cases, the Government's financial participation is expected to be limited to providing land. Where an overlap with public sector entities is unavoidable (for example, in the telephone project where new lines will have to be connected to an existing network operated by a public corporation), the authorities are considering options under which the private sector would undertake the initial construction and afterward lease back the facility, with the public sector getting a share of the revenues.

While the delegation of responsibility for developing infrastructure will certainly moderate the increase in public investment over the medium term, the full macroeconomic implications of large private sector infrastructural projects are as yet unclear, partly because plans have yet to be finalized. In particular, the precise means by which these projects will be financed (domestically or from abroad), and the resulting impact on external debt, the current account, and aggregate demand, are all unresolved issues that will need to be carefully considered.

Tax Reform

Thailand's revenue/GDP ratio has grown markedly since the first half of the 1980s, increasing by over 4 percentage points to close to 20 percent of GDP in 1989/90. As such, the level of revenue mobilization compares favorably with most other countries in the region (Table 6) and, more important, has been more than sufficient to meet the spending needs of the Government. Accordingly, the emphasis in tax reform is not so much on further increasing revenue mobilization (though this may be needed if public sector investment expands substantially), as on developing a more efficient tax structure. In this regard, three issues dominate the agenda of tax reform in Thailand.

Foremost among these is the proposed replacement of the business tax by a value-added tax (VAT). The shift, which has until recently been delayed by a lack of political consensus, has been motivated as much by

Box 5. Infrastructural Issues

Thailand's rapid economic growth has placed increasing strains on the physical infrastructure, particularly in the areas of transportation, telecommunications, power supply, water supply, and port capacity. These bottlenecks are at present concentrated in the Bangkok Metropolitan Region, where much of the recent development has taken place; but substantial infrastructural investment will also be needed in connection with the Eastern Seaboard project, which is already well advanced, and the Southern Seaboard project, still at the planning stage.

Since 1989 public investment in infrastructure has been substantially increased; in the future, however, the private sector is expected to play an increasing role. Projects currently under consideration are

- Roads, railways, and mass transit. Traffic conditions in Bangkok continue to deteriorate, with the average traffic speed down to 10 kilometers an hour, and chronic traffic jams commonplace; public transportation remains very limited. Thus, a series of projects to improve public transport are envisaged: the Skytrain (an elevated light railway); the Hopewell community train and urban freeway project; and a light train system in the central business district proposed by the Bangkok Metropolitan Authority. The highway system in Bangkok will also be extended, including a toll road to Don Muang Airport, and the second and third stages of the expressway system. A fourth stage, which will link Bangkok with 19 key provinces, is currently being studied.
- Seaports and airports. Some 90 percent of Thailand's external trade passes through the Klong Toey Port, which has become increasingly congested owing to the boom in Thailand's trade and to the limited space available for further expansion. As part of the Eastern Seaboard project, new ports are being built at Laem Chabong (whose first terminal opened in 1991) and at Mab Ta Phut (where the first phase will be completed by 1992). A second Bangkok international airport, supplementing Don Muang Airport, which is expected to reach capacity by the year 2000, has also recently been approved.
- Telecommunications. With only 1.3 million telephone lines, and a waiting list of over 1 million customers (which is increasing at three times the rate new lines are currently being installed), the shortage of telephone lines in Thailand has become an urgent problem. In October 1990, the previous Cabinet approved a B 150 billion project that would increase the number of available lines by 3 million by 1997, to be built and operated under a 25-year lease by the Charoen Pokphand Telecommunications Company. Following a review by the new Government, the number of telephone lines to be installed has been reduced to 2 million only in the Bangkok metropolis. The other 1 million for rural areas will be open for bidding shortly. The Transport and Communications Ministry has also recently approved a commercial satellite project, to be implemented by the Shinawatra Computer Group, under which two satellites with telecommunications, broadcasting, and mobile phone capabilities will be launched, beginning in the first quarter of 1993.
- Utilities. Electricity demand has surged over the past five years, with the result that the power reserve (the percentage by which production capacity exceeds demand) has fallen below the standard minimum level of 15 percent. With a substantial increase in investment in new capacity by the Electricity Generating Authority of Thailand (EGAT) in both 1990 and 1991, however, capacity is expected to increase by over 50 percent by 1993, bringing the power reserve well above the minimum level, and thereafter to increase broadly in line with demand. Several projects are also under way to reduce water shortages, particularly in Bangkok, which have led to a series of environmental and health problems (see Box 4).

While improved infrastructure is seen as essential, the authorities view the ultimate solution as decentralizing development away from the Bangkok Metropolitan Region. With the development of the Eastern Seaboard, this has already started to some extent; and growth in the regions should be further stimulated by the proposed Southern Seaboard—a 180-kilometer "land bridge" of highways, railways, and pipelines linking the Gulf of Thailand to the Andaman Sea. It is also expected that the investment incentives administered by the Board of Investment—currently under review—will in the future be primarily aimed at boosting regional development.

the desire to increase tax efficiency as to improve tax compliance. The authorities estimate that, after allowing for various exemptions (such as on food and other essential products), a 10 percent tax rate will be required to ensure that revenues from the VAT fully offset the loss of business tax receipts. The administrative machinery required to implement the tax is already in place, and the measure now only awaits legislative approval; full implementation is expected in January 1992.

A second major item on the agenda is a proposed reduction in import tariffs, which are still judged to be somewhat high (see Section V for a full discussion). The authorities also plan to eliminate a number of other indirect taxes, mainly "nuisance taxes" such as the exit tax (a holdover from earlier times when budgetary exigencies necessitated a number of ad hoc measures).

Third, the authorities are considering overhauling income and corporate taxes to bring the tax structure closer in line with other countries in the region (Table 6). Income tax reform is expected to include further reductions in the number of tax brackets and the level of marginal tax rates. Corporate tax rates may also be cut, although the emphasis here is likely to be on reducing and rationalizing the large number of exemptions that distort the incentive structure. The revenue

Table 6. Regional Comparison of Revenue Performance and Tax Rates, 1989[1]
(In percent)

	Revenue/GDP	Marginal Income Tax Rates	Corporate Tax Rates
Three developing countries			
Thailand[2]	18.0	5–55	30–35
Malaysia	25.4	5–45	35
Indonesia	17.5	15–35	25–35
Four NIEs			
Korea	16.7	5–50	20–33
Singapore[3]	30.1	4–33	32
Taiwan Province of China[4]	14.2	22–40	15–25
Hong Kong	16.8	3–25	16.5
Japan	14.3	10–50	26–40

Sources: Price Waterhouse, *Worldwide Summary of Individual and Corporate Taxes*, 1990; International Monetary Fund, *International Financial Statistics*, and Fund staff reports; and Taiwan Province of China, *Financial Statistics*.
[1]Calendar-year basis, except where noted.
[2]The top marginal tax rate in Thailand was reduced to 50 percent in February 1991.
[3]Fiscal year ended March 31, 1990; ratio to GNP.
[4]Fiscal year ended June 30, 1989.

impact of these changes in direct taxes is expected to be modest.

Size of Fiscal Surplus

By themselves, the requirements for higher capital expenditure (the increase in which will be moderated by private sector participation) and, to some extent, tax reform[13] both work to reduce the fiscal surplus. The extent to which a reduction in the fiscal surplus is desirable hinges on the overall macroeconomic situation. In the short term, in the absence of a clear indication that domestic demand growth is slowing to more sustainable levels, a strong case can be made for maintaining a tight stance of fiscal policy. Over the longer term, the appropriate stance of fiscal policy will depend on the needs of macroeconomic balance, particularly taking into account the expected step-up in investment (including the infrastructural projects discussed above), and the extent to which these can be financed by increases in private savings.

[13] The impact of tax reform on revenues must, however, be judged in a dynamic rather than a static framework. For instance, while the immediate impact of a reduction in import duties would be to reduce revenues, the subsequent increase in imports could result in higher tariff revenues over the longer term.

IV Financial Reform

Over the past two decades, Thailand's financial system has more than tripled, with the ratio of financial assets to GDP increasing from 40 percent to 120 percent. But while the financial sector is now quite deep,[14] it still has a long way to develop. In common with many other developing countries, it is dominated by a relatively small group of domestic banks; the variety of financial instruments available to both users and providers of funds is limited; and, with the important exception of the stock market, the capital markets remain quite thin. To address these shortcomings, the authorities are currently preparing a wide-ranging program of financial reforms, with the threefold aim of boosting savings to support future growth; enhancing the capability of the financial sector to compete in international markets; and ultimately promoting Thailand as a regional financial center.

The Financial System

Financial Institutions

The financial system consists of the Bank of Thailand; 32 banks, including 29 commercial banks and 3 specialized banks owned by the Government; 94 finance and securities companies; several government-owned or sponsored specialized institutions; and a large number of small private and publicly owned institutions (Table 7).

The commercial banking sector, which accounts for 71 percent of total financial assets, dominates the financial system. Most domestic banks were originally established by business groups and trading houses to help finance their operations, and they maintain close links today. The 15 local commercial banks, with their extensive branch networks, account for more than 95 percent of bank assets; the 14 foreign banks, which are subject to a number of restrictions,[15] account for only 5 percent. The banking system itself is highly concentrated, with the 5 largest domestic banks accounting for some two thirds of total bank assets; new entry is highly restricted, with only 1 new bank established in the last twenty-five years.

The second largest group of financial institutions are the 94 finance and securities companies, which account for some 14 percent of total financial assets. They emerged originally in the early 1960s as affiliates of commercial banks either to provide services that the parent bank could not undertake directly or to engage in higher-margin but higher-risk consumer finance, and subsequently expanded into certain types of corporate finance. After a period of dramatic expansion in the 1970s, partly reflecting efforts to evade controls imposed on commercial banks, their growth slowed during the 1980s, following financial crises in both 1979 and 1983 (see Box 6 for a description of the latter). Finance and securities companies are forbidden from offering checking accounts and derive their funding from sales of promissory notes, which can be withdrawn on demand. Their activities cover short-term finance, hire purchase, underwriting and security trade, and other investment and advisory services, most of which commercial banks are not permitted to undertake; they are not yet allowed to undertake foreign exchange business, which is reserved to the commercial banks.

The remaining financial institutions account for about 15 percent of financial assets. Chief among these are the various government-owned financial institutions, particularly the Government Savings Bank, which aims to mobilize primarily household savings through an extensive branch network; the Bank for Agriculture and Agricultural Cooperatives (BAAC), which makes loans to the agricultural sector; and the Government Housing Bank, which helps persons of moderate income to purchase houses. The other financial institutions include the Industrial Finance Corporation of Thailand (IFCT), a privately owned development bank financed primarily through foreign borrowing (with government guarantee);[16] a large number of savings and agricultural

[14] While comparable data on the share of financial assets to GDP are not available, the ratio of broad money (M2) with respect to GDP in 1989 was 67.4 percent in Thailand, 68.2 percent in Malaysia, 35.2 percent in Indonesia, 93.2 percent in Singapore, and 41.2 percent in Korea.

[15] Foreign banks are disadvantaged with respect to domestic banks in three respects: they are prohibited from opening new branches; being subsidiaries of parent companies, they are not juristic entities, so cannot be quoted on the stock exchange, and thus are ineligible for the concessional 30 percent corporate tax rate; and they pay a withholding tax on dividends transferred overseas.

[16] The Ministry of Finance does, however, still hold some shares in IFCT.

Table 7. Financial Institutions

			Assets (in billions of baht)									
			1970		1975		1980		1985		1990	
	Year Started	Number	Amount	Percent	Amount	Percent	Amount	Percent	Amount	Percent	Amount	Percent
Bank of Thailand	1942	1	30.31		56.23		142.72		223.93		478.37	
Banks		32	51.29	94.6	141.97	80.4	362.62	79.6	813.34	80.5	2,017.01	80.0
Commercial banks	1888	29	43.16	79.6	121.83	69.0	307.21	67.4	716.28	70.9	1,799.45	71.4
Specialized banks		3	8.13	15.0	20.14	11.4	55.41	12.2	97.06	9.6	217.56	8.6
Government Savings Bank	1946	1	6.82	12.6	14.15	8.0	27.97	6.1	54.89	5.4	134.62	5.3
Bank for Agriculture and Agricultural Cooperatives	1966	1	1.31	2.4	5.18	2.9	17.33	3.8	28.47	2.8	52.08	2.1
Government Housing Bank	1953	1	...	...	0.81	0.5	10.11	2.2	13.70	1.4	30.86	1.2
Nonbank financial institutions		2,667	2.94	5.4	34.50	19.6	93.07	20.4	196.50	19.5	502.86	20.0
Finance and securities companies	1969	94	...	...	23.00	13.0	64.79	14.2	130.96	13.0	343.14	13.6
Credit foncier companies	1969	18	...	...	1.29	0.7	4.10	0.9	4.46	0.4	4.26	0.2
Small Finance Corporation of Thailand	1964	1	0.05	0.1	0.06	...	0.06	...	0.06	—	0.08	—
Industrial Finance Corporation of Thailand	1959	1	0.44	0.8	1.48	0.8	4.15	0.9	14.96	1.5	36.57	1.5
Savings cooperatives	1946	827	0.69	1.3	1.72	1.0	4.42	1.0	15.18	1.5	56.02	2.2
Agricultural cooperatives	1916	1,357	0.79	1.5	3.22	1.8	5.92	1.3	8.17	0.8	10.01	0.4
Pawnshops	1866	357		—	1.51	0.9	3.18	0.7	5.07	0.5	7.81	0.3
Life insurance companies	1929	12	0.97	1.88	2.22	1.3	6.45	1.4	17.64	1.7	44.97	1.8
Total[1]		2,699	54.23	100.0	176.47	100.0	455.69	100.0	1,009.84	100.0	2,519.87	100.0
Assets/GDP *(percent)*			39.8		59.1		69.2		99.6		121.2	

Sources: Data provided by the Thai authorities; and IMF staff estimates.
[1]Excludes the Bank of Thailand.

cooperatives; credit foncier companies (which finance the purchase of immovable assets); life insurance companies; and pawnshops.

Financial Markets

The main financial instruments available to individuals are bank deposits, promissory notes issued by the finance and securities companies, and shares. On the borrowing side, the primary sources of finance are loans from the banking system or from the finance and securities companies, share issues, and, for larger companies, foreign borrowing. Government bonds and Treasury bills, the other main financial instruments available, have recently been in short supply owing to the Government's sizable fiscal surplus, and are mainly held by the banks to satisfy various portfolio requirements. While other financial instruments do exist—for instance, commercial paper, transferable certificates of deposit, short-term notes, debentures, and floating rate notes—they have in practice played only a limited role.

Overall, the primary market for debt instruments has shrunk steadily since 1985 to a level of 5.6 percent of M2 at end-1990 (Table 8). In part, this contraction is due to the absence of an active market in government paper, which typically precedes the development of a market in corporate paper because individual corporate issues are too small to develop a secondary market of sufficient size to support the necessary institutional infrastructure; but it also reflects legal restrictions on the issuance of long-term debt[17] by corporations.

The two main short-term markets are the interbank market, through which the larger retail banks supply funds to smaller banks and finance companies, and the repurchase market for government bonds operated by

[17] Only those companies that are listed or approved by the Securities Exchange of Thailand (SET), and companies awaiting acceptance for their securities to be listed on the SET, are allowed to issue long-term debt. As discussed further below, this situation will change in due course with the introduction of the much awaited Securities and Exchange Commission.

Box 6. The 1983 Financial Crisis

In October 1983, Thailand experienced a financial crisis, triggered initially by large losses in a finance company and its affiliates. This was eventually to spread to one third of its financial institutions, accounting for about one fourth of total financial assets. In the following three years 24 financial institutions had their licenses revoked, and the Bank of Thailand was forced to intervene in some 30 more. The crisis, which was aggravated by a slowdown in growth and a tightening of monetary policy, brought to the fore widespread pressures in the banking system and particularly among the more loosely controlled finance companies. At the same time, the injection of liquidity that was necessary to support failing institutions complicated the conduct of monetary policy and the achievement of macroeconomic stabilization objectives. These pressures included weak management practices (notably the extension of credit and guarantees to businesses with which bank directors and shareholders were involved, and an overconcentration of lending to a few large-scale and interrelated industries) together with weaknesses in the supervisory and regulatory framework. In a successful attempt to maintain confidence in the financial system, the Thai authorities took a variety of measures to support these ailing financial institutions, while at the same time moving to strengthen the legal, regulatory, and supervisory framework. The Bank of Thailand was empowered to enforce compliance with regulations through direct intervention, to order an increase in bank capital, and to remove bank directors and officers when deemed necessary in the public interest; restrictions on transactions between financial institutions and their directors were tightened; and the Bank's powers to conduct on-site examinations were strengthened. Finally, the Fund for the Rehabilitation and Development of Financial Institutions (RF), subsequently renamed the Financial Institutions Development Fund, was established under the aegis of the Bank of Thailand, with the main purpose of rehabilitating financial institutions.

The main elements of support for finance and securities companies were liquidity injections through several schemes, the most important of which was the "lifeboat scheme," set up in April 1984. To join the lifeboat, participating institutions had to agree to write off their losses, provide reserves for doubtful accounts, strengthen credit and collection procedures, suspend dividends, and submit a financial plan for returning the institution to health. In addition, the value of their shares was reduced, and 25 percent of the shares plus 50 percent of the voting rights were to be transferred to the Ministry of Finance. The voting rights were later to be returned to the original owners, at a price to be determined by the Ministry of Finance. Thus, although the ownership of existing shareholders was diluted, they retained the hope of recovering the value of their shares later on. In return, they were eligible for credits at market rates to offset deposit withdrawals; capital injections through equity participation by the Krung Thai Bank; and direct subsidies from the Bank of Thailand in the form of soft loans that had to be invested in government paper. Twenty-five companies joined the lifeboat scheme: as of early 1991, seven still remained in the lifeboat.

The main support arrangements for commercial banks have been government takeover, subsidized loans from the Bank of Thailand and the RF to be invested in government bonds, and equity participation by the RF, combined with a restructuring of the bank's management under Bank of Thailand guidance. As a condition of support, the Bank set financial programs for banks, specifying a path for increases in capital and writing off bad loans; the Bank and the RF also purchased shares in supported institutions so that they would receive part of the benefits of the subsidies provided through increased share values. Overall, 5 banks received financial assistance under these schemes.

the central bank. Beyond this, money markets and long-term debt securities markets are very shallow, and secondary markets are almost nonexistent, the latter owing partly to double taxation of transactions. On the other hand, the stock market, founded in 1975, has grown steadily since recovering from a crash in 1979, with the ratio of market capitalization with respect to GDP rising from less than 4 percent in 1980 to 29 percent in 1990. The unregulated money market also played an important role in the past, but shrank during the 1980s as higher real deposit rates and improved financial services began to be offered in the formal market. Difficulties in the financial sector also increased public awareness of risk and prompted savers to turn to the larger formal institutions.[18]

[18] The increased monetization of the economy from 1982 onward was not reflected in an increase in the private savings ratio, suggesting that it primarily resulted from a shift of funds out of the informal market.

Conduct of Monetary Policy

Monetary policy is guided by targets for a range of monetary aggregates, determined on the basis of the authorities' objectives for inflation, growth, and the balance of payments. The chief monetary policy instruments are open market operations in the repurchase market and lending by the Bank of Thailand. The Bank of Thailand also influences monetary conditions through ceilings on lending interest rates (until recently, on deposit interest rates as well), and through intervention in the exchange market. Reserve requirements exist for prudential purposes, but are not actively used as an instrument of monetary policy.

The primary instrument of monetary policy is open market operations in the repurchase market. Since the central bank acts not only as a participant but also as the sole dealer, it can easily obtain firsthand information and inject or absorb liquidity whenever it judges it

Table 8. Size of Primary Markets
(In millions of baht)

	1980	1985	1986	1987	1988	1989	1990
Debt instruments	23.0	71.9	58.8	60.3	61.5	46.4	85.4
Short-term instruments	8.4	33.3	22.6	24.6	20.3	20.2	44.6[1]
Treasury bills	8.4	12.0	12.0	11.5	2.0	—	25.7[1]
Commercial paper	—	2.4	8.4	11.2	16.7	18.7	17.2[1]
Transferable certificates of deposit	—	18.9	1.9	1.0	0.3	0.2	0.1[1]
Notes[2]	—	—	0.3	0.9	1.3	1.3	1.6[1]
Long-term instruments	14.6	38.6	36.2	35.7	41.2	26.2	40.8
Government bonds	13.1	35.8	31.0	29.0	26.7	13.0	11.3
State enterprise bonds	1.5	1.9	3.6	2.5	2.2	1.8	6.7
Bank of Thailand bonds	—	—	—	—	2.0	—	13.4
Debentures	—	0.3	0.2	2.3	3.2	4.3	2.4
Floating rate notes	—	0.6	1.4	1.9	7.1	7.1	7.0
Equity market (market value)	25.3	49.4	75.1	137.3	221.9	656.7	609.8
Common shares	24.8	48.7	74.2	134.9	218.1	647.3	602.9
Preferred shares	0.1	0.2	0.2	0.4	0.5	2.2	1.7
Warrants	—	—	—	—	—	—	0.5
Unit trusts	0.4	0.5	0.7	2.0	3.3	7.2	4.7
Memorandum items:							
Debt instruments							
As percentage of GDP	3.5	7.1	5.4	4.8	4.1	2.6	4.1
As percentage of M2	9.1	12.1	8.8	7.5	6.4	3.8	5.6
Equities							
As percentage of GDP	3.8	4.9	6.9	11.0	14.7	36.7	29.3
As percentage of M2	10.0	8.3	11.2	17.0	23.2	54.4	39.9

Source: Data provided by the Thai authorities.
[1]As of September 1990.
[2]Issued by Citibank, Chase Manhattan Bank, and the Industrial Finance Corporation of Thailand (IFCT).

appropriate to do so. The eligible securities in this market are government bonds and the form of operation resembles short-term lending and borrowing, with securities functioning as collateral. Until 1986, the central bank's operations in the repurchase market largely involved matching the demand and supply of repurchases, with limited intervention on its own account for monetary control purposes. But, following the substantial improvements in the external position in 1986 and the emergence of a high level of liquidity in the banking system, the central bank actively drained liquidity through government bond repurchases. These operations were supplemented by the introduction of sales of the central bank's own bonds from 1987.[19] Reflecting the growing importance of open market operations, the volume of transactions in the repurchase market increased sixfold between 1980 and 1990 (to B 600 billion).

The Bank of Thailand lends to financial institutions through a general loan window and a refinancing facility. The former provides short-term liquidity with government securities as collateral, and banks must show that they have no alternative source of funds. Reflecting the "last-resort" nature of this window, the outstanding amount was B 2.4 billion at the end of 1990, far lower than the ceiling of B 13.8 billion (1 percent of deposits for each bank) imposed by the Bank of Thailand for monetary control purposes. In 1986, the authorities simplified the scheme by moving from a dual to a unified interest rate. Recently, the Bank of Thailand has begun to change the loan window interest rate more frequently to signal changes in its policy stance.

The Bank of Thailand's refinancing facility is designed to allocate more financial resources to priority sectors,[20] at preferential interest rates by providing

[19] The current government-approved ceiling for Bank of Thailand bond issues is B 30 billion and, as of December 1990, the outstanding amount issued was B 13.4 billion.

[20] Currently, the priority sectors eligible for refinancing are exports (which account for 90 percent of the total), manufacturing, agricultural production, the wholesale trade of agricultural products, stock

credits to commercial banks against their promissory notes. In 1989, this scheme was changed to improve the distribution of financial assistance (which was heavily skewed toward large exporters whose share in total exports was declining) and to lower the direct subsidy provided. The amount that commercial banks could borrow from the Bank of Thailand out of the amount of commercial banks' loans extended under this scheme was lowered from 60–100 percent to 50 percent. At the same time, the preferential interest rate charged by commercial banks to customers was raised from not more than 7 percent to not more than 10 percent a year, while refinancing interest rates remained at 3–5 percent depending on the sector. Additional funds were made available for small-scale industries and rural development. As a result of these measures, the amount of refinancing outstanding declined from B 37 billion at the end of 1988 to B 22 billion at the end of 1990. A global ceiling for the facility, as well as ceilings for individual banks, is set by the Bank of Thailand and reviewed every six months.

Banks are subject to a basic reserve requirement of 7 percent of deposit liabilities, of which at least 2 percent must be held in the form of deposits in the Bank of Thailand, up to 2.5 percent as vault cash, and the remainder can be held as government securities.[21] The reserve requirement has not been actively used as an instrument of monetary policy, and has remained unchanged for the past 20 years. In addition to the basic reserve requirement, commercial banks must hold 7.5 percent of their deposit liabilities (reduced in stages from 16 percent in 1988) in the form of government securities if they wish to be eligible to open new branches.

Financial Reform

Over the past decade, financial reform measures have been implemented primarily in response to specific problems, rather than as part of an overall reform strategy. The measures included a first step toward interest rate liberalization in 1979/80 with the introduction of laws empowering the Minister of Finance to vary the ceilings on interest rates offered by commercial banks and finance companies; the introduction in 1979 of the repurchase market for government paper; and the amendment of the Commercial Banking Act to broaden the ownership of commercial banks.[22] During the remainder of the 1980s, reform efforts concentrated on providing support for financial institutions experiencing difficulties, and particularly on strengthening the supervisory and regulatory framework (see Box 6), and, in 1984, some reforms of the capital market were instituted.[23]

By the end of the 1980s, however, as Thailand's growth and industrialization accelerated, it became increasingly clear that the time had come for a more comprehensive approach. The initial reform effort focused on interest rate liberalization. In June 1989, the interest rate ceiling on time deposits with a maturity of more than one year was lifted to encourage long-term deposit-taking and to enable commercial banks to adjust themselves to a more flexible interest rate system. Subsequently, in March 1990, interest rate ceilings on time deposits with a maturity of one year or less were abolished; currently ceilings remain only on savings deposits and lending rates.

Foreign exchange transactions were also liberalized. In May 1990, the authorities accepted the obligations of Article VIII of the Fund's Articles of Agreement; simultaneously, the scope for commercial banks to approve foreign exchange transactions without seeking prior approval from the Bank of Thailand was increased. A further package of liberalization measures, concentrating on capital account transactions, followed in April 1991. Specifically, foreign exchange earners were allowed to open foreign exchange accounts with commercial banks in Thailand up to $500,000 for individuals and $5 million for corporations. Thai investors could freely transfer up to $5 million abroad for direct investment. The package also permitted free repatriation of investment funds, including dividends and loan repayments, without the prior approval of the Bank of Thailand. The remaining restrictions are limited to resident purchases of property, financial instruments, and equity abroad, which are subject to prior approval by the Bank of Thailand.

The authorities are now preparing a three-year plan that encompasses a broad range of liberalization meas-

financing for agricultural exports, and rural development. The export sector has been the major beneficiary of the facilities owing to the more systematic trade documentation system which needs to be presented for access to the facility, compared with other sectors.

[21] The Bank of Thailand requires finance and securities companies to maintain a liquidity asset ratio, which is similar—but less onerous in terms of interest forgone—to the reserve ratio for commercial banks, owing to the nature of their fund mobilization (through promissory notes). The current liquidity asset ratio is 7 percent and may be fulfilled in the form of a balance at the Bank of Thailand, which must be no less than 0.5 percent, government bonds (no less than 5.5 percent), and deposits at commercial banks or call loans to these banks (up to 1 percent).

[22] The maximum individual shareholding was limited to 5 percent and it was established that banks should have at least 250 shareholders. In addition, the Ministry of Finance was given the power to suspend temporarily part or all of a commercial bank's operations.

[23] The Securities Exchange of Thailand Act was amended mainly to prohibit all insider-trading activities. The new Act also allowed listed companies and SET-approved companies, as well as limited companies whose securities were still under consideration for acceptance by the SET, to issue new debentures to the public. Prior to the amendment, only listed companies had been permitted to do so. In 1985, as an inducement to go public, a different income tax rate was applied to listed companies—30 percent—compared with 35 percent for unlisted companies. In 1986, two foreign funds were established, namely, the Bangkok Fund and the Thailand Fund, to encourage portfolio investment from abroad. Warrants and convertible debentures were introduced in 1988.

ures. They view comprehensive reform as urgently needed not only to strengthen the efficiency of the financial system to cope with future challenges and international competition, which could intensify along with an agreement in the Uruguay Round of the General Agreement on Tariffs and Trade (GATT), but also to support the fast-growing real sector without creating bottlenecks. At the same time, the authorities consider that the ability of financial intermediaries to absorb reforms has greatly increased in recent years; the old managerial style of family control has been replaced by professional management teams; most banks and a number of finance and securities companies have increased their capital adequacy, and their portfolio quality has improved; and the profitability of financial institutions has risen sharply. While a detailed blueprint for further financial reforms has not been issued, some elements have been referred to in official pronouncements, and these are described below.

Restructuring Commercial Banks and Finance and Securities Companies

The authorities' strategy entails (i) a widening of the scope of business of these institutions in line with the international trend toward a universal type of banking system to promote domestic institutions' competitiveness vis-à-vis foreign banks; and (ii) a reduction of entry barriers to promote fair competition among financial institutions. As regards the former, the Bank of Thailand has forwarded recommendations to the Government to expand the activities of commercial banks and finance and securities companies, whereby commercial banks would be allowed to underwrite debt instruments—both private debt and government and state enterprise securities—and undertake leasing and provident fund management and provide investment advice. Finance companies would be allowed to expand into areas previously reserved for the commercial banks. Foreign exchange business would be permitted for some finance companies that demonstrate sound management with an adequate capital base. As a result, the top-tier finance companies would, in actuality, become commercial banks. For securities companies, additional business such as custodial services and registrant and agent for dividend payments would be authorized. As to the latter, the Bank of Thailand proposes to introduce more competition in the banking sector by allowing new foreign banks to operate in Thailand, although implementation of measures in this area will be linked to a successful conclusion of the Uruguay Round.

The Bank of Thailand also intends to introduce measures to improve the quality of securities and finance companies partly by encouraging mergers between those companies that are not sufficiently competitive. Since mergers appear to be difficult under the current merger law—which requires the 100 percent agreement of creditors before mergers can take place—the authorities are considering introducing a new legal framework that would regulate mergers and acquisitions. They believe that merger incentives for small and medium-sized finance companies will be considerable, since amount of capital would be the most important criterion in selecting financial companies allowed to undertake foreign exchange transactions. In addition to encouraging mergers among finance companies, permission to establish joint ventures with foreign partners is also being considered as a long-term measure.

Further Deregulation

In the relatively near term, the authorities plan to abolish the remaining interest rate restrictions on both banks and finance companies. (The limit on the savings interest rate will entail modification of existing legislation.) They are also considering eliminating the remaining portfolio constraints on banks, namely, the requirements of government bond holding for branch opening and on the share of lending to the rural sector.[24]

Strengthening Prudential Supervision

The authorities intend to continue strengthening prudential supervision to ensure the stability of the financial system in the context of liberalization. In particular, they intend to emphasize the importance of capital adequacy, which would be brought into line with levels recommended by the Bank for International Settlements. Asset quality would also be stressed, with the requirement that risk-based capital be properly disclosed.

As regards the equity market, legislation is being prepared to set up a separate and independent institution along the lines of the U.S. Securities and Exchange Commission (SEC) to supervise the stock exchange. At present, the supervisory power is vested in a number of government departments: the Ministry of Finance has the power to approve stocks to be listed on the SET; the Bank of Thailand supervises finance and securities companies; and the SET Board regulates the operations of the stock exchange. The establishment of an independent body would facilitate the supervision of both primary and secondary trading.

Developing Financial Instruments and Markets

As previously noted, the debt instrument market—short-term money markets and long-term bond (non-equity) markets—is not well developed. The Bank of

[24] Currently, commercial banks are required by the Bank of Thailand to lend at least 20 percent of their previous year's deposits for rural activities. An amount equivalent to any shortfall of lending from the target must be deposited in the Bank for Agriculture and Agricultural Cooperatives.

Thailand plans to promote the development of new financial instruments through measures in four main areas. First, the legal barrier to the issuance of debt instruments and the transaction tax on secondary trading of financial instruments would be eliminated. Second, the planned elimination of the government bond holding requirement for branch openings also will help develop secondary markets for government bonds. Third, private companies would be encouraged to issue debt instruments to the public directly, after instituting appropriate prudential safeguards. Finally, to improve the financial infrastructure, the telecommunications system is to be expanded, and the establishment of a credit rating agency is being considered.

Improving Payments and Information Management System

As a measure to improve the efficiency of the payments and financial information system, the authorities plan to introduce a system of electronic transfers to facilitate payments in both wholesale and retail transactions. The system, which will be centralized at the Bank of Thailand, will enable commercial banks to review their financial positions on a real-time basis. Further, the authorities will encourage greater use of checks and credit cards to reduce the dependence on cash.

V Trade Policies

(Intro to trade)

From the beginning of its modern economic history, Thailand has traditionally maintained an open trade and exchange system, which has contributed to its economic success. From the late 1950s, although Thailand embarked on industrial development through an import-substituting strategy, tariff rates ranging from 15 percent to 30 percent remained low in comparison with most other developing countries. However, during the 1970s, even as the emphasis of industrial policy swung increasingly toward export promotion, tariff rates were increased substantially, doubling the average rate of effective protection in the course of the decade.[25] The increases in tariff rates partly reflected the policy response to increasing balance of payments difficulties; they were accompanied by a proliferation of exemptions on specific products and by surcharges and nontariff barriers.

From the early 1980s, a reversal of this buildup of trade barriers became an important policy goal. Considerable progress was made in reducing nontariff barriers, including the proportion of goods subject to import restrictions, and the use of specific import surcharges by the Board of Investment to protect domestic industries also declined sharply. But, partly owing to fiscal constraints, less progress was made in reducing the level of tariffs, although their dispersion fell somewhat over the period: while many minor tariff reductions were implemented, the structure of tariffs remained broadly unchanged.[26] Since early 1990, however, as part of a wide-ranging program of economic liberalization, policy initiatives in trade reform have been renewed, as described in more detail below.

Structure of Nominal Tariffs and Effective Protection in the 1980s

Between 1981 and 1985, the overall tariff level, as measured by the unweighted average tariff rate, remained broadly unchanged, although the dispersion of the tariff declined (Tables 9 and 10), owing largely to the reduction of almost all tariff rates to 60 percent or less in 1982. Actual import duties collected as a percentage of imports, particularly for capital goods, were lower than the weighted average tariff, mainly reflecting the various tax exemptions available from the Board of Investment (see Section II), as well as the duty drawback schemes available for exporters (see below). A feature of Thailand's tariff structure, shared with many other developing countries, was "tariff escalation," whereby the average level of the tariff increased with the degree of processing of the product: raw materials were typically subject to very low, and finished products to relatively high, rates of duty. Thus, effective protection was considerably higher than that implied by the nominal tariff rates.

Since calculations of effective rates of protection are based on a variety of theoretical and empirical assumptions,[27] the results can vary considerably according to the methodology used. But while individual results must be interpreted with care, they can provide useful information about the impact of the tariff system on producers' decisions and thus on the structure of domestic production.

Estimates of the effective rate of protection during the period suggest that the average rate of protection in Thailand is quite high, owing primarily to the tariff escalation during the 1970s and the tariff increases of 1985 (Tables 9 and 11).[28] At the same time, the wide dispersion of nominal tariff rates has also led to a wide

[25] The effective rate of protection measures the percentage by which value added at domestic prices (taking into account the effect of tariffs and other protective measures) exceeds value added at world prices. See Corden (1971) for a full discussion of the concept.

[26] In 1982, the maximum tariff rate on almost all products (except for a few luxury items, including automobiles) was reduced to 60 percent, and a variety of other tariffs were also reduced; the impact of these measures, however, was largely offset by the simultaneous imposition of a 10 percent temporary surcharge on import duties for revenue reasons. In 1984, this surcharge—after first being raised to 20 percent—was eliminated on all but a few products: but in early 1985, tariffs on raw materials and intermediate goods were raised by 5 percent, and on finished goods by 10 percent, again to boost revenues.

[27] The concept of the effective rate of protection is based on a number of crucial assumptions, including perfect competition, perfect substitution between domestic and imported commodities, fixed coefficient production, and no substitution between industries. Calculations of the effective rate of protection are also complicated by the need for a high degree of aggregation and the difficulties of obtaining input-output data. See Corden (1971) for details.

[28] Based on calculations by Bhattacharya and Brimble (1986) and updated by World Bank staff through 1988.

Table 9. Tariff Rates and Effective Protection

	September 1981	March 1983	October 1984	November 1984	April 1985	January 1988
Nominal tariffs						
Unweighted	31.0	32.6	32.8	29.9	33.8	. . .
Standard deviation	(30.1)	(28.6)	(28.7)	(26.3)	(27.3)	. . .
Weighted[1]	14.3	16.2	16.6	15.3	18.5	. . .
Effective protection						
Unweighted	66.7	66.4	65.3	59.0	65.9	64.6
Standard deviation	(140.2)	(140.4)	(136.7)	(131.3)	(132.0)	(131.4)
Weighted[2]	27.9	27.9	28.5	25.5	30.0	29.7

Source: World Bank staff estimates.
[1]By 1985 import values.
[2]By 1980 value added at world prices.

dispersion of effective protection rates across industries, although reduced slightly by the tariff reforms during the 1980s. Frequent changes in tariff rates on individual products during the 1980s also resulted in substantial variations in effective protection rates for individual industries over time (for instance, the effective rate of protection on flour varied from 89 percent to 164 percent between 1981 and 1985).

The protective system has strongly favored the manufacturing sector relative to both agriculture and the production of other primary products (Table 11). Within the manufacturing industry, effective protection rates vary widely, being highest for finished consumer goods and lowest for intermediate and capital goods. The tax exemptions available from the Board of Investment for imports of intermediate and capital goods, which are not taken into account in the calculations, are likely to exacerbate this divergence.

The anti-export bias inherent in any tariff system has been reduced in Thailand by various export promotion schemes. Since 1958, the Bank of Thailand has operated an export rediscount facility, providing short-term loans to exporters at subsidized interest rates; and since the early 1970s, export orientation has been increasingly important in determining the distribution of investment incentives. In addition, the operation of the various duty drawback schemes, which refund tariffs and business taxes on imports used to produce exports, has

Table 10. Tariff Structure

	Weighted Nominal Tariff	Average Rate of Import Duty[1] 1985	1990
Consumer goods	24.8	25.4	18.0
Intermediate products	14.1	12.1	8.5
Raw materials	5.1		
Capital goods	22.3	12.7	9.9
Automotive products	63.0	44.8	42.5
Total	18.5	14.0	11.8

Sources: World Bank staff estimates; and data provided by the Thai authorities.
[1]Calculated as import duties in percent of import value.

Table 11. Structure of Effective Protection[1]

	April 1981	January 1988
Agriculture	10.9	13.1
Other primary products	5.7	11.3
Agroprocessing	24.7	32.9
Other manufacturing	53.6	51.2
Textiles	(110.4)	(59.9)
Chemicals	(49.3)	(9.5)
Machinery	(18.9)	(35.2)
Consumer goods	(51.5)	(68.7)
Overall average	27.9	29.7

Source: World Bank staff estimates.
[1]Effective protection rates weighted by share in 1980 value added at world prices.

Table 12. Manufacturing Industry Classified by Sales Orientation and Effective Protection Rate (ERP), 1985

	Negative Protection		Positive Protection		Total	
	Number of sectors	Mean ERP	Number of sectors	Mean ERP	Number of sectors	Mean ERP
Exporting sectors	7	−15	24	122	31	91
Import-competing sectors	2	−13	43	61	45	58
Noncompeting sectors	3	−4	10	39	13	29
Nontrading sectors	—	—	1	32	1	32
Total	12	−12	78	77	90	65

Source: IMF staff estimates.

been significantly improved since the early 1980s; and institutional support to exports (such as export marketing and trade fairs) has been strengthened.[29]

A recent study by Bhattacharya and Lin (1988) compared Thailand's nominal tariff structure with those of a group of its East Asian neighbors.[30] While it found that Thailand's average nominal tariff was the highest among the countries in the sample, Thailand also had a relatively low level of nontariff barriers, including quantitative restrictions. Overall, the study concluded that Thailand's protective system was broadly comparable to those in Indonesia and the Philippines; Korea and Malaysia, however, appeared to have somewhat less restrictive regimes. The study also observed that the level and dispersion of nominal protection in all five countries was much lower than in most developing countries in Latin America and South Asia.

Trade Liberalization in 1990 and Beyond

Given Thailand's small domestic market, its prosperity and growth must rest primarily on its ability to export, and since the early 1970s export promotion has assumed a greater role in its industrial strategy. As Thailand prepares for accelerated industrial development in the 1990s, the distortions created by the tariff structure could have an increasingly damaging effect. Tariff reform, therefore, has become more important in the authorities' program of market liberalization.

As a first step, in October 1990 tariffs on capital goods used in manufacturing were reduced from 20 percent to 5 percent, and the tariff exemptions or reductions on these goods that could previously be granted by the Board of Investment were abolished.[31] This should not only simplify both the tariff and the investment incentive system, but should also particularly benefit small exporting firms that profit less from Board of Investment incentives. The authorities have recently stated their intention to enact a second package of tariff reforms during 1991, which is expected to include reductions in tariffs on raw materials, intermediate products and certain capital goods, and some finished products, aimed particularly at benefiting exporters and exporters' suppliers who have been unable to gain from Board of Investment exemptions or to participate in the various duty drawback schemes. This potentially represents a further important step toward lowering the level and the dispersion of effective protection, and thereby increasing efficiency.

[29] Also, an analysis of the structure of effective protection in the manufacturing sector by sales orientation suggests that overall the export sector had a higher rate of effective protection than the import-competing sector, partly because some important exporting sectors (such as textiles) started off as import-competing industries and expanded into exports as the domestic market became saturated (Table 12). While this would not, of course, help these industries on the world market, such industries could benefit through relatively high profits on their domestic production. Competitive conditions in the domestic market would also play a role.

[30] The countries in the sample were Thailand, Indonesia, Korea, Malaysia, and the Philippines.

[31] The goods covered are principally under Sections 84 and 85 of the Customs Tariff. Items not covered include consumer and business electronics, transportation equipment such as automotive engines, and certain items that can be produced domestically such as air conditioners. The Board of Investment retains the ability to grant exemptions on business and local taxes on these items.

P

Export Promotion (EO EI)

VI The Economy in a Regional Perspective

After four consecutive years of rapid growth (averaging over 11 percent a year), moderate inflation, and record balance of payments surpluses, Thailand has emerged as one of the most dynamic economies in the world today. While there are special factors at work that are unique to Thailand, it is difficult to ignore its location in a region that has become synonymous with economic dynamism. In seeking such a regional perspective, this section takes a broad view of the term "region" to include both a core of neighboring developing countries (Thailand, Malaysia, and Indonesia) and an outer circle of the more advanced economies of Japan and the four NIEs: Hong Kong, Korea, Singapore, and Taiwan Province of China. Two concentric notions of the term are needed because the shared experiences and policy issues in the core developing region have been shaped by developments in the outer circle of East Asia's more advanced economies. In particular, the latter have not only been an important source of expanding trade, but have also, in response to structural changes in their own economies, become major investors in the core region.

The choice of countries here is as much defined by an underlying similarity in economic policies as it is by geography. Clearly, the common denominator has been the pursuit of an outward-oriented growth strategy supported by cautious financial policies, arguably the central forces behind the region's impressive economic record.[32] In this respect, the recent experience of Thailand differs from that of the more advanced outer circle economies more in timing than in substance. Like the NIEs in the 1970s, and like Japan a decade before, Thailand has used the high savings rate associated with rapid economic growth to finance a step-up in domestic investment, especially in export-oriented industries, rather than to run trade surpluses, thereby sustaining export-led growth over time. The investment and export boom of recent years is not unique to Thailand and may also be found, in greater or lesser degree, in Malaysia and Indonesia, giving rise to a similar (but not identical) set of macroeconomic policy issues.

[32] Important differences in the degree and nature of import protection afforded to various sectors across the region remain.

Common Policy Issues in the Core Region

While the countries of the core region share the common features of geographic proximity and a rich endowment of natural resources, they are scarcely a homogenous economic zone. There are important differences in per capita incomes and economic structure (Table 13): for example, Indonesia and Malaysia, but not Thailand, are large oil exporters, and Indonesia's population is more than three times that of Thailand, and ten times that of Malaysia. Differing economic priorities therefore prevail. For example, reducing the dependence of government revenues and exports on oil and gas is a key objective of economic policy in Indonesia and a somewhat lesser objective in Malaysia, whereas it is obviously not an issue in Thailand. Nevertheless, while bearing such factors in mind, it is instructive to focus on the substantial commonality of experience and policy issues encountered in these three economies.

Thailand, Malaysia, and Indonesia each emerged from a difficult period in the mid-1980s only after implementing major adjustment programs. The global recession and downturn in commodity prices in the early 1980s adversely affected growth, inflation, and export earnings in the three countries. In Malaysia and Thailand, persistent fiscal deficits contributed to a weakening in their external positions, and to a buildup in external debt. Indonesia attempted to adjust to the external shocks by curtailing government expenditures; however, because of an even larger decline in oil revenues, larger government deficits were incurred and were financed by external borrowing. Compounding these problems was the large cumulative loss in export competitiveness resulting from the strong links of the three currencies to the appreciating U.S. dollar during the first half of the 1980s.

They all responded promptly to adverse developments with strong adjustment measures. The type and mix of policies varied, but in general they were designed to increase economic efficiency, improve domestic resource mobilization, and diversify the structure of production and exports. In Malaysia and Thailand, the focus was on fiscal adjustment, with fiscal balances

Table 13. Regional Economic Indicators, 1989

	GDP *(in billions of U.S. dollars)*	GDP per Capita *(in U.S. dollars)*	Average GDP Growth (1985–89)	Share of Manufacturing in GDP[1]	Exports *(in billions of U.S. dollars)*		Imports *(in billions of U.S. dollars)*	Ratio of Exports/ GDP	Ratio of Savings/ GDP[2]	Ratio of Investment/ GDP	Foreign Direct Investment *(in billions of U.S. dollars)*
Core region											
Thailand	69.7	1,257	8.6	24.1	20.1	(—)	25.8	29.1	27.5	31.1	1.7
Malaysia	37.5	2,210	4.6	25.1	25.0	(3.6)[3]	22.5	66.8	29.2	29.6	1.9
Indonesia	94.0	525	5.5	18.4	22.2	(8.7)[3]	9.3	23.6	33.6	34.7	1.0
Four NIEs											
Korea	211.9	5,000	9.8	33.7	61.4		56.8	29.0	36.9	34.5	0.5
Singapore	28.4	10,582	6.0	28.7	43.2		45.7	152.1	43.6	35.4	4.0
Taiwan Province of China	146.9	7,307	9.9	35.6	66.1		52.5	45.0	30.6	22.8	−5.3
Hong Kong[3]	62.9	10,916	8.9	19.1	73.1		72.5	116.3	34.7	26.7	. . .
Japan	2,833.7	23,016	4.5	27.4	269.6		192.7	9.5	34.3	31.5	−45.2

Sources: International Monetary Fund, *International Financial Statistics*; Fund staff reports; and Taiwan Province of China, *Monthly Statistics*.
[1]Percentage share of GDP at current prices, except for Malaysia, Thailand, and Korea whose shares are at constant prices. Hong Kong's share is based on 1988 data.
[2]Savings data refer to national savings, except for Hong Kong where a domestic savings concept is utilized.
[3]Oil and gas exports.

improving in each by close to 6 percent of GDP during 1986–88. In Indonesia, there was a more fundamental shift toward an outward-oriented growth strategy (already a feature of policies in Malaysia and Thailand), and the key measures included fiscal retrenchment, tax and financial reforms, and the progressive deregulation of trade and industry. Exchange rate devaluation was a feature of all three programs, an objective aided by the fall of the U.S. dollar following the Plaza Accord.

Adjustment efforts were hampered in each country by deteriorating terms of trade. Nevertheless, perseverance with adjustment policies began to yield results that, in turn, poised all three countries to take advantage of the improved international setting that ensued from 1986. By about 1987, they entered a period of economic expansion, driven by exports and private investment. Total fixed investment increased substantially in the core region, most notably in Thailand and Malaysia, where it rose by about 7 percent of GDP in 1987–89 (Chart 7). Foreign direct investment, much of it export oriented, was an important force behind the step-up in investment during this period, accounting for about 15 percent of the increase in Thailand, and close to 40 percent in Malaysia. Correspondingly, exports also grew rapidly, with the shift from primary commodities to manufactured goods accelerating markedly (Chart 8). Manufactured exports more than doubled in value and volume terms between 1987 and 1990, and now account for the bulk of exports in both Thailand and Malaysia. As a result, all three economies became steadily more industrialized, as reflected in the rising shares of manufacturing in output and exports. In 1989 manufacturing accounted for about one fourth of GDP and about one half of exports in Malaysia and Thailand; the shares for Indonesia were slightly smaller, at 19 percent and 24 percent, respectively.

Not surprisingly, the similar origins of their success have given rise to similar problems. Booming investment since 1988 has led to demand pressures that have raised inflation (most obviously in Indonesia and Thailand) and contributed to a decline in the current account balance (Chart 7). The latter development has, to a large extent, reflected rising imports of construction materials and machinery and equipment (Chart 8). Also associated with such demand pressures has been the growing prominence of infrastructural bottlenecks in the region. This phenomenon has attracted most attention in Thailand, where it is feared that shortages in skilled labor, power, water, transport, and communications could act as a brake on foreign direct investment as well as slow down the economy's growth momentum. In response to these developments, a number of efforts have been initiated to alleviate such bottlenecks, including greater private sector involvement in the provision of basic infrastructure (see Section III). In Indonesia too, shortages in the power sector have become serious, and the authorities are considering plans for investments entailing private sector participation, along the same lines as in Thailand. Malaysia, by contrast, has thus far avoided major bottlenecks, but the heightened pace of economic growth in recent years has prompted the authorities to target an expansion in

Chart 7. Macroeconomic Trends in Core Region, 1985–90

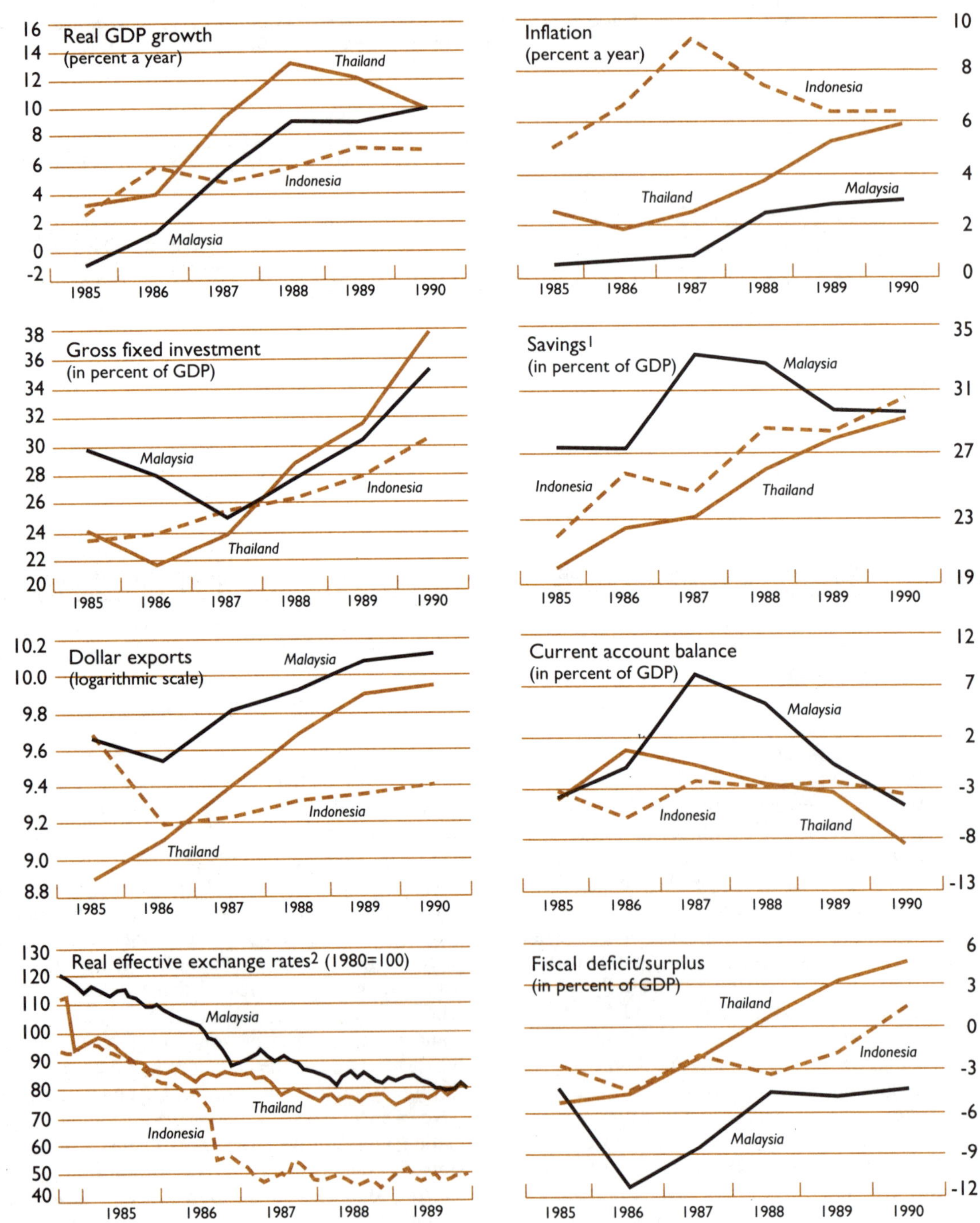

Source: Data provided by the Indonesian, Malaysian, and Thai authorities.

[1]In view of large variations in inventories and statistical discrepancies, national savings is defined here as gross fixed investment plus the current account balance.

[2]Decline in index indicates depreciation.

Chart 8. Composition of Trade,[1] 1986-89

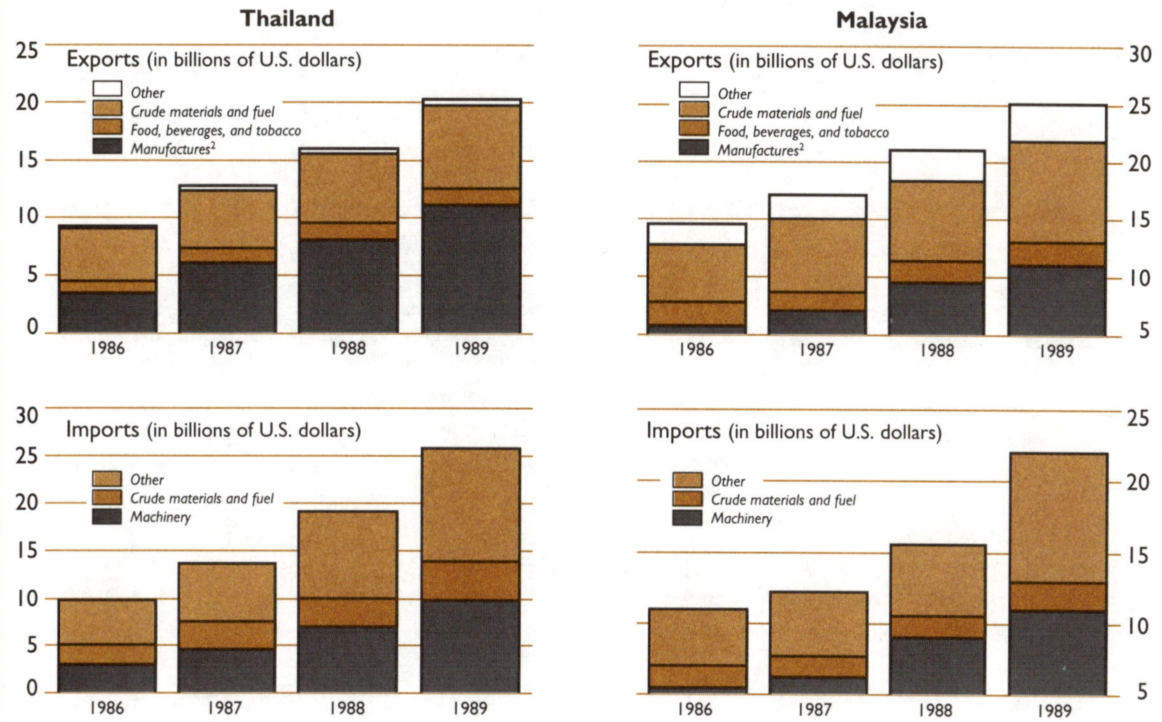

Source: Data provided by the Thai and Malaysian authorities.
[1]Customs data classified by Standard International Trade Classification. Indonesia is not included here for lack of data on a comparable basis.
[2]Manufactured goods, machinery, transportation equipment, and miscellaneous manufactures.

infrastructure and spending on human resources as a central goal of fiscal policy over the medium term.

Despite rising current account deficits, the overall balance of payments has been in substantial—and still rising—surplus in both Thailand and Malaysia (Indonesia, by contrast, has recorded overall deficits since 1988). While the bulk of net capital inflows into Malaysia have been in the form of foreign direct investment, Thailand has relied primarily on foreign borrowing. In both cases, the sheer volume of capital inflows has greatly complicated the task of restraining monetary growth. For example, net capital flows into Thailand in 1989 exceeded in value the stock of reserve money at the start of the year. As a result, monetary aggregates have tended to grow ahead of the authorities' original targets.[33]

In all three countries, the authorities have assigned the task of restraining domestic demand to fiscal policy, with an improved public sector performance playing a major role in checking the increase in the overall savings-investment gap (Chart 7). This trend has been particularly marked in Thailand, where chronic deficits during the first half of the decade have since given way to large and growing fiscal surpluses, achieved primarily through considerable restraint in both current and capital spending (including a cautious approach that avoided proceeding with large projects until the need for them was clearly demonstrated), but also reflecting buoyant revenue growth, partly a by-product of the booming economy.[34] In Malaysia too, the public sector deficit declined appreciably during the second half of the 1980s. However, the burden of adjustment fell primarily on development spending, where the cutbacks were

[33] The deeper question of the ability of the monetary authorities to sterilize such inflows obviously hinges on the degree of capital mobility. Appendix I discusses this issue for Thailand.

[34] The process of fiscal consolidation in Thailand is described in greater detail in Section III.

Table 14. Regional Trade of Core Developing Countries, 1980–90[1]

	1980	1981	1982	1983	1984	1985	1986	1987	1988	1989	1990
						(In millions of U.S. dollars)					
Regional trade											
Thailand	5,720	6,422	5,995	7,049	7,410	6,779	7,383	10,043	14,843	19,904	25,684
Malaysia	11,132	11,745	13,071	14,346	16,328	14,996	12,656	15,724	19,064	24,257	31,288
Indonesia	19,649	21,022	25,535	22,129	19,780	15,867	13,947	16,589	17,883	20,754	23,943
Regional exports											
Thailand	2,480	2,582	2,498	2,355	2,493	2,450	3,245	4,037	5,582	7,023	7,985
Malaysia	6,395	6,364	6,918	7,858	9,156	8,828	7,410	9,387	10,702	12,585	15,545
Indonesia	14,170	14,624	15,332	13,640	13,853	11,735	9,066	10,590	11,966	13,514	14,891
Regional imports											
Thailand	3,240	3,840	3,497	4,694	4,917	4,329	4,158	6,006	9,261	12,881	17,699
Malaysia	4,738	5,382	6,154	6,488	7,082	6,167	5,245	6,337	8,361	11,672	15,743
Indonesia	5,479	6,399	8,203	8,489	5,928	4,132	4,882	5,999	5,917	7,240	9,052
						(Percentage share of total)[2]					
Regional trade											
Thailand	36.4	37.9	38.7	42.3	41.7	41.4	40.9	40.6	41.0	43.7	46.3
Malaysia	46.9	50.4	53.4	52.4	53.2	54.4	51.3	51.4	50.7	50.9	53.1
Indonesia	60.0	59.2	60.1	59.0	55.3	55.0	52.1	55.3	54.7	54.0	53.8
Regional exports											
Thailand	38.1	36.8	36.0	37.0	33.6	34.4	36.3	34.4	35.0	34.9	35.3
Malaysia	49.4	54.1	57.5	55.7	55.5	57.7	53.6	52.4	50.7	50.2	52.7
Indonesia	64.7	65.7	68.8	64.5	63.2	63.1	56.4	61.8	61.5	61.6	60.6
Regional imports											
Thailand	35.2	38.7	40.9	45.6	47.4	46.8	45.3	46.2	45.7	50.7	53.9
Malaysia	44.0	46.6	49.5	48.9	50.4	50.3	48.5	50.0	50.6	51.7	53.6
Indonesia	50.6	48.2	48.7	51.9	42.7	40.3	45.5	46.5	44.7	44.0	45.3
						(In percent of total trade)					
Memorandum items:											
ASEAN trade[3]											
Thailand	13.8	13.0	14.3	14.2	15.2	16.6	14.2	14.6	11.9	11.8	13.0
Malaysia	17.7	19.9	21.4	20.3	20.3	20.9	18.7	19.7	19.5	19.6	21.7
Indonesia	11.6	12.3	16.8	19.0	12.0	9.8	9.3	10.7	9.7	9.5	5.7

Source: International Monetary Fund, *Direction of Trade Statistics.*
[1]Trade between core countries and with Korea, Singapore, Taiwan Province of China, Hong Kong, and Japan.
[2]Respectively, in percent of each country's total trade (exports plus imports); exports; and imports.
[3]Trade with the Association of South East Asian Nations: Brunei, Indonesia, Malaysia, Philippines, Singapore, and Thailand.

sufficient even to offset a substantial fall in the ratio of revenues to GDP. The same was also true for Indonesia, although the magnitudes have been somewhat smaller. If infrastructural investment is targeted to recover in these countries (led by the private sector in Thailand, and by the public sector in Malaysia and Indonesia), they must now confront the implications for the overall savings-investment gap as a central issue for the medium term.

Regional Interdependence

What role has the region played in generating the fundamental forces—investment and exports—that have impelled Thailand, Malaysia, and Indonesia toward record growth rates? Clearly, since trade and investment between these countries is small,[35] the answer must lie within a wider regional grouping that includes the more advanced NIEs—Korea, Singapore, Taiwan Province of China, and Hong Kong—and Japan. On this basis, the region is indeed significant for the core developing economies.

The statistics on trade are revealing. Table 14 confirms that regional trade grew dramatically during the 1980s in dollar terms, particularly in Thailand (where it multiplied fivefold) and in Malaysia (where it nearly tripled).[36] While regional trade has declined

[35] For example, Thailand's trade with Malaysia and Indonesia accounts for less than 4 percent of the total; similarly, direct investment flows from the latter were less than 1 percent of the total in 1989.

[36] Table 14 should be interpreted with care, since the data are

slightly in relative importance—as measured by trade shares—in Malaysia and Indonesia, it nevertheless continues to account for well over half of total trade. On the other hand, the importance of regional trade to Thailand grew steadily through the 1980s. Underlying this trend has been a greater reliance on the region not so much as an export destination but as a growing source of imports, particularly from Japan (Chart 9).[37] This is not really surprising, given the investment-driven nature of demand growth in the core region, and Japan's pre-eminent position as one of the world's leading suppliers of capital and machinery (so that *all* countries in the region—even the NIEs—run bilateral trade deficits with Japan). The strong link between capital goods imports and foreign direct investment (both dominated by Japanese companies) has also been an important factor in the growth of imports from Japan.

Although foreign direct investment is hardly new to the region, the magnitude of recent inflows sets it apart as a distinct and increasingly important factor. While foreign direct investment has doubled in Indonesia in recent years, it is, quantitatively, most significant in Thailand and Malaysia. Again, it has been investment flows from the NIEs and Japan—accounting for over two thirds of total foreign direct investment in Thailand and Malaysia in recent years—that has driven foreign direct investment to unprecedented levels in these countries (Tables 15 and 16).[38] The major impetus to foreign direct investment in the core region has come from higher wage costs and exchange rate appreciation in the NIEs and in Japan, as well as in response to rising international protectionist pressures, all of which have worked to encourage plant relocations away from the advanced East Asian economies. For their part, Thailand, Malaysia, and Indonesia have been able to attract such investment by virtue of their low labor costs, financial and political stability, and a traditional commitment to outward-oriented policies and to the private sector. In Thailand, as in Malaysia and Indonesia, these plant relocations have been focused on the tradable goods sector, including consumer electronics, household appliances, computer equipment, and toys. A major implication of this pattern of investment is that, insofar as these facilities replace production earlier undertaken in the NIEs, export growth is less constrained by overall growth in the world economy. In this sense, regional foreign direct investment has helped sustain the growth momentum in the core region even as world economic growth has slowed. The next phase in the product cycle, only just under way, is the relocation of lower value-added industries from Thailand to neighboring countries, including Myanmar, the Lao People's Democratic Republic, and Viet Nam.

However, saying that regional foreign direct investment is important is not the same as saying that the foreign direct investment is equally important in every case. It must be measured particularly against the overall level of savings and investment in the economy, where a crucial difference emerges. Although foreign direct investment has grown in importance relative to domestic investment, it still accounted for only about 8 percent of total investment in Thailand in 1989, whereas it was as high as 17 percent in Malaysia. Indeed, foreign direct investment accounted for nearly 40 percent of the total increase in investment in Malaysia in 1987–89. Similarly, total foreign direct investment was only 27 percent of net capital inflows into Thailand in 1989, but was 129 percent in Malaysia. A slowdown in foreign direct investment would therefore have a relatively smaller impact on aggregate demand and on the capital account of the balance of payments in Thailand than it would in Malaysia.

Even so, there is little doubt that all the developing countries of the core region attach great importance to foreign direct investment flows and, moreover, actively compete with one another for it in a variety of ways. Although tax incentives are frequently given prominence, their role in attracting foreign investment is not generally regarded as primary. Other factors such as wage competitiveness, availability of skilled labor, and adequate infrastructure are considered to be more important. While it is in these areas that the developing countries of the core region are expected to compete in the coming years, it should be recognized that such competition does not preclude cooperation. A recent example is the joint development of export centers in Johore (Malaysia) and Bataam (Indonesia) by Malaysia, Indonesia, and Singapore.

Regional Cooperation

Formally, Thailand's involvement in regional cooperation has proceeded mainly under the aegis of the Association of South East Asian Nations (ASEAN), which consists of Brunei, Indonesia, Malaysia, the Philippines, Singapore, and Thailand. To date, ASEAN has functioned more as a political forum than as an economic one, although the latter role has been growing since the late 1970s. Economic cooperation has been evident in two principal areas. Preferential trading

partly distorted by entrepôt trade with Singapore and Hong Kong. The lack of data on a comparable basis precludes a correction for such transactions.

[37] Although Thailand's exports are less concentrated on East Asia than either Malaysia's or Indonesia's, its regional exports have grown markedly in dollar terms, while its regional export share has remained steady at a little over one third of total exports. Correspondingly, Thai exports are more dependent on North American and European Community (EC) markets.

[38] As with trade data, the figures here need to be interpreted cautiously, since what is classified as "regional investment" may in fact be investment undertaken by regional affiliates of multinational corporations.

Chart 9. Pattern of Trade in Core Region, 19850–90
(In billions of U.S. dollars)

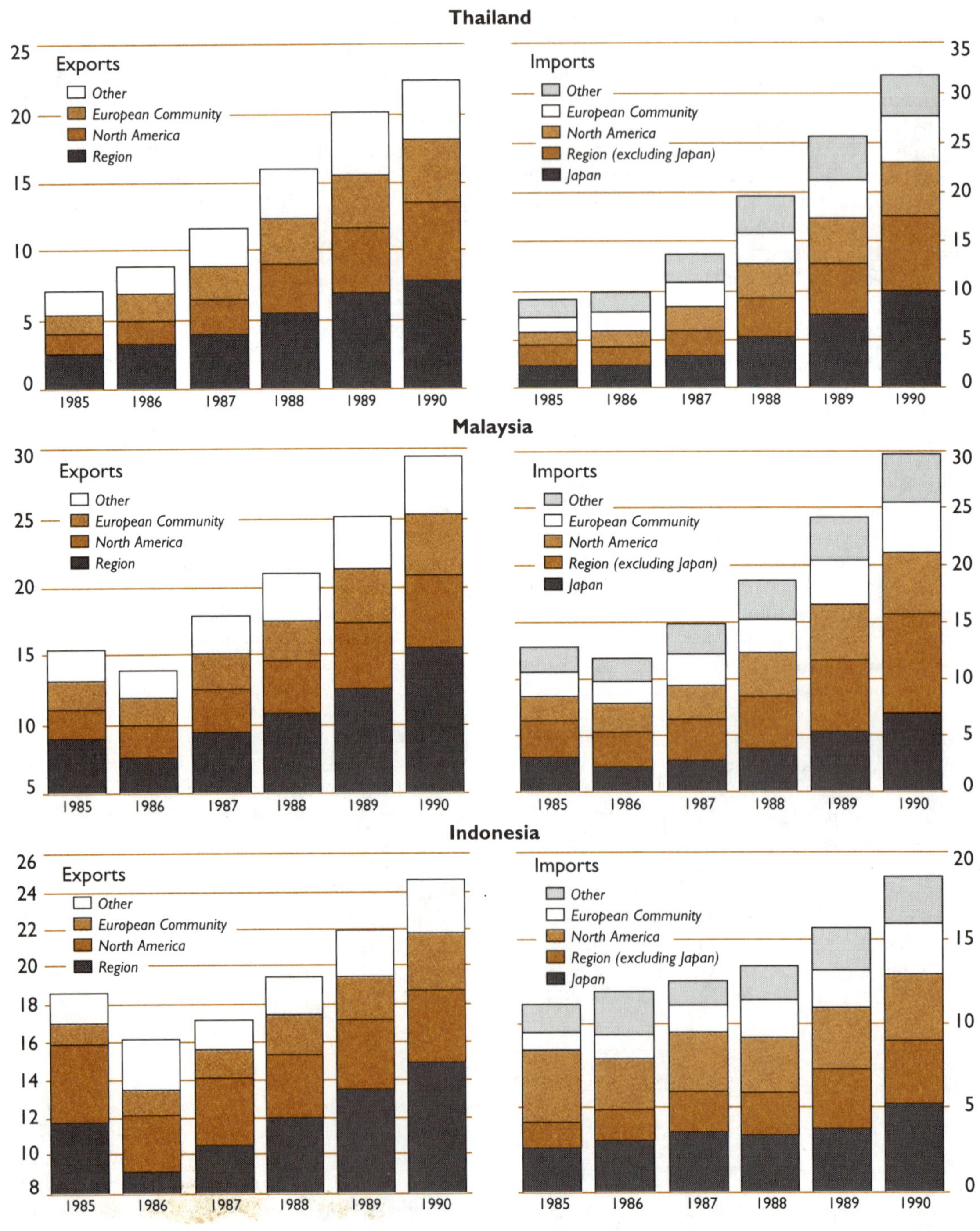

Source: International Monetary Fund, *Direction of Trade Statistics.*

Table 15. Foreign Direct Investment in Core Region, 1985–89

	1985	1986	1987	1988	1989
			(In millions of U.S. dollars)		
Total foreign direct investment					
Thailand	162	261	182	1,082	1,650
Malaysia	695	489	423	719	1,846
Indonesia	310	258	385	576	682
Total investment					
Thailand	8,982	9,075	11,655	17,180	21,646
Malaysia	8,605	7,207	7,234	9,013	11,102
Indonesia	24,495	22,630	23,814	26,532	32,639
			(Percentage ratio)		
Total foreign direct investment/total investment					
Thailand	1.8	2.9	1.6	6.3	7.6
Malaysia	8.1	6.8	5.8	8.0	16.6
Indonesia	1.3	1.1	1.6	2.2	2.1
Total foreign direct investment/GDP					
Thailand	0.4	0.6	0.4	1.8	2.4
Malaysia	2.2	1.8	1.3	2.1	4.9
Indonesia	0.4	0.3	0.5	0.7	0.7
Memorandum items:					
Total foreign direct investment/net capital flows					
Thailand	9.9	45.3	9.6	28.0	26.5
Malaysia	36.2	35.5	−38.0	−25.1	128.8
Indonesia	13.1	18.0	9.9	80.3	73.3

Source: International Monetary Fund, *International Financial Statistics*.

Table 16. East Asian Foreign Direct Investment in Core Region, 1989
(Share of total foreign direct investment)

	Thailand[1]	Malaysia[2]	Indonesia[3]
A. Four NIEs	30.4	34.4	19.0
Korea	0.5	1.1	. . .
Singapore	7.9	10.6	3.1
Taiwan Province of China	9.5	17.9	8.1
Hong Kong	12.5	4.8	7.7
B. Japan	42.2	30.3	19.5
C. East Asia (A + B)	72.5	64.7	38.4
D. Other	27.5	35.3	61.6
E. Total	100.0	100.0	100.0

Sources: Bank of Thailand; Bank of Indonesia; and Bank Negara Malaysia.
[1] Actual foreign direct investment, cash basis (which differs from *IFS* data).
[2] Approvals basis, data averaged 1987–89.
[3] Approvals basis, data averaged 1987–89; excludes Korea, for which data were not available separately.

arrangements, allowing for lower tariffs on intra-ASEAN trade in selected goods, were initiated in 1977 and subsequently expanded to cover some 15,000 goods. However, because of substantial exclusions in individual countries, as well as the focus on lightly traded goods with low price elasticities, the volume of trade under such preferential arrangements has remained small (about 2 percent of intra-ASEAN trade in 1987)—see Rieger (1989) for further details. A number of schemes—including the ASEAN Industrial Projects (AIP), ASEAN Industrial Complementation (AIC), and ASEAN Industrial Joint Ventures (AIJV)—were begun in the late 1970s and early 1980s to exploit economies of scale in the region. These programs—covering areas such as fertilizers, automobile parts, and pharmaceuticals—have included both equity participation from member governments as well as tariff incentives going beyond what is available under the general preferential tariff arrangements. The number of projects under these schemes has been limited, however.

Overall, the importance of ASEAN for trade and investment has been small for most of its members (Table 14). In practice, particularly for Malaysia, intra-ASEAN trade has amounted to trade with Singapore, partly reflecting the latter's position as the regional center of entrepôt trade: in Thailand, intra-ASEAN trade (about 15 percent of the total) and intra-ASEAN investment (about 8 percent of the total) are also dominated by Singapore. Accordingly, ASEAN may be more important as a forum for collectively voicing the concerns of this group of small and relatively open economies on global economic issues, particularly on world trade. The Thai authorities, in particular, have stressed the importance of an open trading system and have expressed their strong commitment to the success of the Uruguay Round of the GATT.

The objective of promoting regional economic cooperation was strengthened in 1989 with the formation of the Asia Pacific Economic Cooperation Council (APEC), which, in addition to Thailand and the other ASEAN countries, also includes Australia, Canada, Japan, Korea, New Zealand, and the United States. The group aims at lowering trade barriers between APEC members, in a manner consistent with the GATT, while at the same time opposing protectionism worldwide. It is thus hoped that regional economic cooperation will evolve from being primarily a reflection of growing trade and investment links to becoming a cause for economic integration. More recently, partly in response to the slow progress in completing the Uruguay Round of trade talks, Malaysia proposed a third grouping—the East Asian Economic Group—consisting exclusively of East Asian countries. While discussions are still under way on the membership and the precise means by which it would promote free trade in the East Asian region, there is general agreement that the organization should also promote the aims of the GATT.

Appendix I Capital Mobility and Monetary Policy

During both 1989 and 1990, the growth of the monetary aggregates in Thailand was driven almost entirely by a rapid increase in private capital inflows, which the Bank of Thailand has found increasingly difficult to sterilize. This difficulty has, in part, reflected the limitations of the monetary instruments available to it, discussed in more depth in Section IV. But the scope for monetary policy has also been constrained by the authorities' policy of fixing the value of the baht to a basket of foreign currencies, which has in practice been reflected in a close link between the baht and the U.S. dollar.

The degree to which the fixed exchange rate is, in fact, a constraint on monetary policy depends critically on the openness of the capital account. In general, the capital account in Thailand has been quite open in recent years (especially for inflows), although there have been important limitations in two areas. First, for prudential reasons the net open foreign exchange position of commercial banks is constrained, thus limiting the degree to which banks can adjust their foreign exchange positions to offset changes in monetary policy.[39] Second, residents have until recently been unable to hold foreign-exchange-denominated deposits in domestic banks; at the same time, there have been controls on capital outflows. This, in turn, is likely to have limited the scope for arbitrage by residents in response to interest rate differentials on domestic and foreign assets. The degree of capital mobility may also be affected by a variety of other factors, in particular the degree of integration between foreign and domestic markets and between domestic markets themselves, even when no formal legal constraint exists: for example, while the largest corporations can reportedly borrow abroad quite easily, this is less likely to be so for other firms.[40]

This appendix assesses the openness of the capital account in Thailand, using a method first put forward by Edwards and Khan (1985), and an extension suggested by Haque and Montiel (1990), and thereby draws some conclusions on the likely effectiveness of monetary policy.

Theoretical Background

The Edwards and Khan approach attempts to measure the openness of the capital account directly by viewing the observed domestic interest rate at time t, i_t, as a weighted average of the interest rate i_t^* that would obtain if the economy was completely open (which would be the foreign rate, adjusted for expected exchange rate changes, risk premiums, and transactions costs) and the interest rate i_t^c that would exist if the economy was completely closed (which would equal expected inflation plus the real interest rate, the latter varying with domestic monetary conditions). Thus, they derive the following equation:

$$i_t = \Psi i_t^* + (1 - \Psi)\, i_t^c. \qquad (1)$$

The parameter Ψ measures the degree of openness of the economy in the long term: if $\Psi = 1$, the economy is fully open. In practice, even in a fully open economy, domestic interest rates may only adjust to foreign interest rates with a lag, reflecting, for example, transactions costs and information lags. To allow for this, the model is extended so that the open economy interest rate adjusts to foreign interest rates with a speed of adjustment Θ (if $\Theta = 1$, then adjustment is instantaneous), allowing a distinction between the openness coefficient in the short run ($\Theta\Psi$) and in the long term (Ψ). The degree of monetary disequilibrium, which determines the real interest rate in a closed economy, can be proxied in several ways. One, embodied in equation (2) below, is to define it as the ratio between real money supply m_t and money demand, the latter a function of real GDP (y_t), the long-run real interest rate (assumed constant) and expected inflation (π^e). A second approach, based on Makin (1982), is to postulate that nominal interest rates are affected in the short run by monetary "surprises." Incorporating these additions, equation (1) can be written

[39] The net liability position is limited to $5 million or 20 percent of capital, whichever is larger; the net asset position is limited to $5 million or 25 percent of capital, whichever is larger. It should also be noted that banks cannot lend in foreign-exchange-denominated instruments.

[40] In theory, small firms could seek foreign loans with a guarantee from a domestic bank, but such guarantees are also covered by the limit on the net open position of banks.

Table 17. Estimations Using the Edwards-Khan Approach

1978: Q2 1990: Q4	Lagged Interest Rate	Foreign Interest Rate	Real GDP	Lagged Money Balances	Monetary Surprise	Expected Inflation	$\bar{R}^2$	DW
Ordinary Least Squares								
1. Standard specification	0.46	0.55	0.98	0.24	—	−0.09	0.76	2.0
	(4.9)	(4.9)	(0.2)	(0.1)		(0.6)		
2. Monetary surprise	0.43	0.54	—	—	−0.32	−0.16	0.78	1.83
	(5.0)	(6.1)			(1.9)	(1.1)		

Source: IMF staff estimates.
Note: The figures in parentheses are *t*-statistics.

$$i_t = d_0 + d_1 i_t^* + d_2 \log y_t + d_3 \log m_{t-1} + d_4 \pi_t^e + d_5 i_{t-1}, \quad (2)$$

where the d_i are parameters. A detailed derivation of this equation, and expressions for the d_i in terms of the underlying parameters of the system, can be found in Edwards and Khan. It is enough to note here that the openness coefficient Ψ is the sum of the parameters d_1 and d_5, while the speed of adjustment Θ can be derived by dividing d_1 by $(d_1 + d_5)$.

This basic approach was adapted by Haque and Montiel for use when a domestic interest rate series either did not exist, or was not fully representative (because, for example, of interest rate controls or other forms of financial repression). Their approach is based on the assumption that the (unobservable) true domestic interest rate is an argument of a conventionally defined money demand function. This money demand function could then be used to substitute for the domestic interest rate in equation (1). The closed economy domestic interest rate could be derived in a similar fashion, assuming that the closed economy money supply m_t equaled the observed money supply *less* the inflow of private capital during the period. On this basis, the following reduced form can be derived

$$\log m_t = a_0 + a_1 i_t^* + a_2 \log m_t^c + a_3 \log y_t + a_4 \ln m_{t-1} + a_5 \pi_t^e. \quad (3)$$

Once again, the detailed derivation can be found in Haque and Montiel; it is sufficient here to note that the openness coefficient Ψ equals $(1 - a_2)$.

Empirical Results

For Thailand, the key interest rates include the interbank and repurchase rates (which in practice move closely together and are the proximate target of monetary policy) and commercial bank deposit and lending rates. However, consistent data series are available only for the first two; lending and deposit rates are not only difficult to define consistently over time, but have also been distorted by the effect of lending and deposit rate ceilings.[41] Therefore, the Edwards and Khan approach was applied to the interbank interest rate series, to assess how far the Bank of Thailand is able to influence the liquidity conditions in the banking system; the Haque and Montiel approach was used to test how far the (unobservable) true marginal cost of funds in the economy is influenced by foreign interest rates.

The two models were estimated using quarterly data for 1978–90; a quarterly GDP series was provided by the authorities through 1988 and extended through 1990 by applying the seasonal factors in the past to the annual data. Given the stability of the nominal exchange rate against the U.S. dollar over most of the period, the expected exchange rate change (against the U.S. dollar) was set at zero[42]: expected inflation was proxied by actual inflation. Changes in these specifications produced no substantive changes in the results.

The results of the estimations of the Edwards and Khan approach are set out in Table 17, using both equation (2) above and a formulation incorporating the effect of monetary surprises.[43] Dummy variables were included for the first quarter of 1985 (in which the interbank rate rose very sharply partly as a result of the depreciation of the baht in November 1984) and for the third quarter of 1990 to take account of the Middle East crisis. Both specifications fit reasonably well, and a Chow test cannot reject the hypothesis of parameter

[41] Indirectly, of course, the ceilings on lending and deposit rates will also have affected the interbank rate.

[42] While there is a forward exchange market in Thailand, transactions in it are restricted, and so the forward premium (or discount) is not a good measure of exchange rate expectations.

[43] The monetary surprise variable was defined as the residual obtained from regressing monetary growth on its past seven lagged values.

Table 18. Estimates of the Openness Coefficient

Equation	Long Run	Short Run
Edwards and Khan (standard specification)	1.01	0.55
Edwards and Khan (monetary surprise)	0.97	0.54
Haque and Montiel	0.59	0.45

Source: IMF staff estimates.

stability. In each case, the lagged domestic interest rate and the foreign interest rate are correctly signed and highly significant; moreover, their values are almost the same in each specification. The long-run openness coefficient Ψ is very close to unity in each case (Table 18), which suggests that the limits on the net foreign position of commercial banks have not been a binding constraint over the period. However, adjustment is not instantaneous, with only about one half of the difference between domestic and foreign interest rates eliminated in each quarter, suggesting that information lags and other sources of friction in the system are important in the short term.

The coefficients of the variables describing domestic monetary disequilibria are generally less well specified, which is perhaps unsurprising given the high value of the openness coefficient noted above. In the standard specification, the coefficients on real GDP, lagged money balances, and inflation are all insignificant, and the coefficient on lagged money balances has the wrong sign. The monetary surprise approach gives generally better results: the coefficient on the monetary surprise is correctly signed and significant at the 5 percent level, although the coefficient on inflation is both insignificant and incorrectly signed.[44]

The results of the Haque and Montiel approach are set out in Table 19. The closed-economy money supply was defined as the money supply excluding all private capital inflows, except direct investment, which is unlikely to be as responsive to changes in interest differentials as other forms of capital inflows. Since a number of variables in the Haque and Montiel equation are nonstationary, the equation was estimated using error correction techniques. To this end, equation (3) was first estimated using ordinary least-squares techniques. The residual series from that estimation passed a standard Dickey-Fuller test for rejection of nonstationarity, and was then used (with a lag of one period) as an argument of an error correction model. The ordinary least-squares estimate can be interpreted as providing the long-run relationship, while the error correction mechanism shows the short-term dynamics. Thus, the long-run openness coefficient can be derived from the ordinary least-squares estimate, and the short-run openness coefficient from the error correction specification.

The estimations in Table 19 fit well, with all variables correctly signed, and all but the foreign interest rate in the ordinary least-squares estimation significant at the 1 percent level: once again, a Chow test cannot reject the hypothesis of parameter stability. The long-run openness coefficient is approximately 0.6, while the short-run coefficient is about 0.5. The short-run openness coefficient is, surprisingly, only slightly lower than that derived using the Edwards and Khan approach, suggesting that those nonbanks that can adjust their portfolios in response to changes in foreign interest rates do so relatively quickly. In the long run, however, the openness coefficient derived using the Haque and Montiel approach is lower than that derived from the Edwards and Khan approach, which confirms the prior expectation that the interbank money market is the most open financial market in Thailand.

Conclusions

On the basis of the above, the following main conclusions can be drawn. First, the results confirm that the Thai capital account is quite open, especially as regards the interbank market. At the same time, both approaches used suggest that the differential between domestic and foreign rates is not eliminated immediately, so that considerable scope exists for an independent monetary policy in the short term. The degree to which this conclusion will hold in the future is, however, less clear. Capital account transactions were further liberalized in April 1991, including the introduc-

[44] Neither of the two estimations using the Edwards and Khan approach satisfactorily predicts the substantial increase in the differential between domestic and foreign rates in 1990, which may also imply that the specification of domestic monetary disequilibria is not fully satisfactory.

Table 19. Estimations Using the Haque-Montiel Approach

Ordinary Least Squares

$$\text{Log } m_t = \underset{(1.1)}{-0.08\, i_t^*} + \underset{(6.3)}{0.41 \log m_t^c} + \underset{(4.2)}{0.14 \log y_t}$$
$$+ \underset{(8.3)}{0.51 \log m_{t-1}} - \underset{(3.3)}{0.53\, \pi_t^e} - \underset{(3.99)}{0.49}$$

$\bar{R}^2 = 0.99$, DW $= 2.0$, H $= -0.1$

Error Correction Model

$$D \log m_t = \underset{(4.2)}{-0.30\, Di_t^*} + \underset{(10.9)}{0.55\, D \log m_t^c} + \underset{(2.5)}{0.13\, D \log m_{t-1}^c}$$
$$+ \underset{(2.3)}{0.07\, D \log y_t} + \underset{(2.5)}{0.07\, D \log y_{t-1}}$$
$$+ \underset{(3.4)}{0.23\, D \log m_{t-2}} - \underset{(4.0)}{0.51\, D\pi_t^e}$$
$$- \underset{(3.2)}{0.44\, D\pi_{t-1}^e} - \underset{(2.1)}{0.31\, res_{t-1}}$$

$\bar{R}^2 = 0.89$, DW $= 1.82$

where res_t is the residual from the ordinary least-squares regression, and D is a difference operator.

Source: IMF staff estimates.
Note: The figures in parentheses are t-statistics.

tion of foreign exchange accounts for corporations and individuals, and the authorities have stated that consideration will be given to eliminating the remaining restrictions on outflows. Moreover, as financial liberalization proceeds, domestic and foreign financial markets will become increasingly closely linked—an important objective of the liberalization program. In the long run, therefore, maintaining a relatively fixed exchange rate is likely to constrain increasingly the conduct of monetary policy.

Appendix II Statistical Appendix

Table 20. Domestic Expenditure and Product
(In billions of baht)

	1980	1985	1986	1987	1988	1989	1990 Est.
	(Percentage change, in 1972 constant prices)						
Consumption	5.0	2.9	3.5	7.3	7.9	9.0	8.1
Private	5.4	2.0	4.3	8.8	8.8	10.9	9.0
Public	2.8	6.9	0.2	0.9	3.5	−0.1	2.9
Fixed investment	3.8	−5.3	−3.8	15.4	21.8	22.0	26.6
Private	−2.6	−11.2	0.5	29.2	32.0	25.6	23.5
Public	18.9	7.6	−11.6	−13.1	−9.4	5.9	43.1
Change in stocks[1]	−0.5	0.2	−0.5	—	2.9	−1.4	0.5
Foreign balance[1]	1.4	2.4	2.5	0.4	0.6	0.9	−2.6
Statistical discrepancy[1]	−1.0	−0.1	1.1	0.4	−0.6	1.2	—
Gross domestic product	4.8	3.5	4.9	9.5	13.2	12.0	10.0
Agriculture	1.7	6.2	0.3	−0.2	10.2	6.6	−3.8
Industry[2]	3.2	−0.9	7.7	12.7	17.8	16.1	15.9
Manufacturing	2.9	−0.6	10.8	13.3	16.8	14.9	14.3
Services	7.0	5.0	5.2	11.2	11.7	11.5	10.7

Source: Data provided by the Thai authorities.
[1]Contribution to GDP growth.
[2]Mining, manufacturing, and construction.

Table 21. Investment and Savings

	1980	1985	1986	1987	1988	1989	1990 Est.
				(As percent of GDP)			
Gross domestic investment	26.4	24.1	21.8	23.9	28.8	31.5	37.8
Private[1]	17.5	15.0	14.2	17.7	23.6	26.3	31.0
Public	8.9	9.1	7.6	6.2	5.2	5.2	6.8
Gross domestic savings	20.9	19.4	20.9	23.7	28.6	30.2	31.4
Private	17.9	16.5	17.1	18.0	19.6	20.3	19.9
Households	10.6	8.9	9.1	9.4	10.6	10.2	9.3
Businesses	7.3	7.6	8.1	8.6	9.0	10.1	10.6
Public	3.0	2.9	3.8	5.7	9.0	9.9	11.5
Statistical discrepancy	−0.9	−0.6	−1.5	0.3	2.5	2.3	2.2
Foreign savings	6.4	4.0	−0.6	0.6	2.7	3.6	8.6

Source: Data provided by the Thai authorities.
[1]Includes change in stocks.

Table 22. Monetary Survey

	1980	1985	1986	1987	1988	1989	1990
				(In billions of baht)			
Net foreign assets	42.4	37.9	80.9	107.6	145.7	247.5	307.1
Net domestic assets	209.4	555.6	591.9	701.0	810.4	959.6	1,222.0
Domestic credit	305.8	697.8	740.7	871.2	1,007.4	1,207.3	1,531.9
Public (net)	85.1	170.5	188.0	190.4	142.7	84.7	35.7
Private	220.7	527.3	552.7	680.8	864.7	1,122.6	1,496.2
Other items (net)	−96.4	−142.2	−148.8	−170.2	−197.0	−247.7	−309.9
Broad money (M2)	251.8	593.5	672.8	808.6	956.1	1,207.1	1,529.1
Narrow money (M1)	71.6	85.9	103.4	132.4	148.5	174.7	195.4
Quasi-money	180.2	507.6	569.4	676.2	807.6	1,032.4	1,333.7
				(Contribution to broad money growth)			
Net foreign assets	4.5	1.8	7.2	4.0	4.0	10.6	4.9
Net domestic assets	17.9	8.5	5.9	16.2	11.4	15.6	21.7
Domestic credit	23.5	10.0	7.2	19.4	14.2	20.9	26.9
Other items (net)	−5.6	−1.5	−1.3	−3.2	−2.8	−5.3	−5.2
Broad money (M2)	22.5	10.3	13.4	20.2	15.4	26.3	26.7
Narrow money (M1)	3.9	−0.5	3.0	4.3	1.7	2.7	1.7
Quasi-money	18.6	10.9	10.4	15.9	13.7	23.5	25.0

Source: Data provided by the Thai authorities.

Table 23. Accounts of the Bank of Thailand

	1980	1985	1986	1987	1988	1989	1990
				(In billions of baht)			
Net foreign assets	55.2	50.1	70.7	106.1	162.4	262.6	360.5
Assets	62.4	80.0	98.6	130.5	179.3	269.7	360.6
Liabilities	7.2	29.9	27.9	24.4	16.9	7.1	0.1
Net domestic assets	2.1	36.4	25.6	10.6	−28.4	−105.9	−174.7
Net claims on Government	54.7	98.0	89.6	83.6	32.2	−22.0	−57.6
Claims on commercial banks	16.5	25.5	34.7	42.0	57.8	41.6	34.6
Claims on other financial institutions	5.4	12.8	14.1	13.6	15.0	16.1	12.6
Other items (net)[1]	−74.5	−101.7	−113.8	−130.5	−135.3	−144.1	−168.1
Reserve money	57.3	86.5	96.3	116.7	134.0	156.7	185.8
				(Contributions to reserve money growth)			
Net foreign assets	−2.4	2.1	23.8	36.8	48.2	74.8	62.5
Net domestic assets	19.4	6.4	−12.5	−15.6	−33.4	−57.8	−43.9
Reserve money	17.0	8.5	11.3	21.2	14.8	16.9	18.6

Source: Data provided by the Thai authorities.
[1]Includes net currency holdings.

Table 24. Balance of Payments Developments

(In millions of U.S. dollars)

	1980	1985	1986	1987	1988	1989	1990 Preliminary
Trade balance	−2,829	−2,219	−494	−1,633	−3,942	−5,358	−9,773
Exports, f.o.b.	6,448	7,077	8,829	11,609	15,857	19,938	22,912
Imports, c.i.f.	−9,277	−9,296	−9,323	−13,242	−19,799	−25,296	−32,685
Of which: Oil	2,868	2,082	1,227	1,710	1,534	2,325	3,053
Services (net)	544	562	569	1,118	2,154	2,697	2,672
Receipts	2,125	3,165	3,336	4,171	5,951	7,052	8,643
Payments	−1,581	−2,603	−2,767	−3,053	−3,797	−4,355	−5,971
Of which: Interest	728	1,233	1,336	1,374	1,435	1,507	1,761
Transfers (net)	216	166	225	225	236	246	206
Of which: Official	142	119	161	125	190	199	182
Current account balance	−2,069	−1,491	300	−290	−1,552	−2,415	−6,895
Nonmonetary capital movements (net)	2,525	1,531	708	808	2,848	5,932	8,182
Medium- and long-term capital (net)	2,525	1,343	321	630	1,245	4,250	3,400
Private sector	1,249	357	82	462	1,530	4,478	4,771
Direct investment	187	198	222	229	995	1,679	2,084
Public sector[1]	1,276	986	239	168	−285	−228	−1,371
Public enterprises	928	605	224	−162	−562	34	435
Central government	348	381	15	330	277	−262	−1,806
Short-term capital	. . .	118	387	178	1,603	1,682	4,782
Errors and omissions[2]	−208	171	714	511	220	672	1,194
Overall balance[2]	273	211	1,722	1,029	1,516	4,189	2,481
Monetary movements	−273	−211	−1,722	−1,029	−1,516	−4,189	−2,481
Commercial banks (net)	−479	−469	−776	243	841	−389	1,576
Monetary authorities[1]	206	258	−946	−1,272	−2,357	−3,800	−4,057
Of which: Net IMF credit	−58	226	−35	−77	−264	−379	−275

Source: Data provided by the Thai authorities.

[1]Excludes $300 million borrowed by the Government in late 1985 to be used for refinancing in the first half of 1986.

[2]Includes counterpart to valuation changes in foreign exchange reserves other than gold amounting to gains of $72 million in 1985, $173 million in 1986, and $368 million in 1987, losses of $58 million in 1988 and $138 million in 1989, and gains of $280 million in 1990.

Table 25. External Debt and Debt Service
(In millions of U.S. dollars; end-of-period data)

	1980	1985	1986	1987	1988	1989	1990 Est.
Total outstanding debt (disbursed)	8,488	17,385	18,171	19,868	20,915	22,700	29,209
Outstanding medium- and long-term debt (disbursed)[1]	6,307	14,158	15,283	16,908	16,167	16,751	18,621
Public sector	4,348	10,528	12,023	13,883	13,035	11,935	11,253
By lender							
IMF[2]	(348)	(1,122)	(1,069)	(973)	(672)	(275)	(1)
International institutions	(976)	(2,979)	(3,175)	(3,193)	(2,889)	(2,761)	(2,698)
Foreign governments	(1,112)	(2,595)	(3,231)	(4,109)	(4,073)	(3,908)	(4,601)
Foreign banks	(1,881)	(3,470)	(4,110)	(5,088)	(4,933)	(4,528)	(3,411)
Suppliers' credits	(31)	(362)	(438)	(521)	(467)	(463)	(542)
By borrower							
Bank of Thailand	(348)	(1,122)	(1,069)	(973)	(672)	(275)	(1)
Central government	(1,463)	(3,516)	(4,292)	(5,160)	(5,281)	(4,940)	(3,689)
Public enterprises	(2,537)	(5,890)	(6,662)	(7,751)	(7,081)	(6,720)	(7,563)
Nonbank private sector	1,752	3,370	3,117	2,837	3,016	4,640	7,368
Loans	(1,463)	(2,952)	(2,731)	(2,448)	(2,510)	(4,104)	(6,619)
Suppliers' credits	(289)	(418)	(386)	(389)	(506)	(536)	(749)
Commercial banks[3]	207	260	143	188	116	176	136
Outstanding short-term debt (disbursed)	2,181	3,227	2,888	2,960	4,748	5,949	10,452
Public sector	60	72	61	66	256	172	257
Nonbank private sector	862	1,851	1,897	1,706	2,274	2,945	6,248
Commercial banks[3]	1,259	1,304	930	1,188	2,218	2,832	3,947
Total debt-service payments	1,444	2,747	2,968	3,080	3,194	3,427	3,307
Amortization	741	1,514	1,622	1,707	1,758	1,920	1,538
Interest	703	1,233	1,338	1,373	1,436	1,507	1,769
Total debt-service ratio[4]	16.7	27.5	24.8	19.8	14.9	13.0	10.9

Sources: Data provided by the Thai authorities; and staff estimates.
[1] Debt with maturity of one year or more.
[2] Includes Trust Fund loans.
[3] Gross foreign liabilities of commercial banks.
[4] As a percentage of exports of goods and services.

Bibliography

Bhattacharya, Amarendra, and Peter Brimble, "Trade and Industrial Policies in Thailand in the 1980s: A Review and a Framework for Policy Reform" (unpublished; World Bank, 1986).

Bhattacharya, Amarendra, and Johannes Lin, *Trade and Industrial Policies in the Developing Countries of East Asia,* World Bank Discussion Paper, No. 27 (Washington: World Bank, 1988).

Bank of Thailand, *Annual Economic Report*, various years.

———, *Quarterly Bulletin*, various issues.

Bunge, Frederica M., ed., *Thailand—A Country Study* (Washington: U.S. Government Printing Office, 5th ed., 1981).

Corden, W.M., *The Theory of Protection* (Oxford: Oxford University Press, 1971).

Edwards, Sebastian, and Mohsin S. Khan, "Interest Rate Determination in Developing Countries: A Conceptual Framework," *Staff Papers*, International Monetary Fund, Vol. 32 (September 1985), pp. 377–403.

Greenwood, John G., "Monetary Policy in Thailand," in *Monetary Policy in Pacific Basin Countries*, ed. by Hang-sheng Cheng (Norwell, Massachusetts: Kluwer Academic Publishers, 1988).

Haque, Nadeem U., and Peter Montiel, "Capital Mobility in Developing Countries—Some Empirical Tests," IMF Working Paper, WP/90/117 (December 1990).

Heller, Peter S., Richard D. Haas, and Ahsan H. Mansur, *A Review of the Fiscal Impulse Measure*, IMF Occasional Paper 44 (Washington: International Monetary Fund, May 1986).

Hutaserani, Sugarya, "The Trends of Income Inequality and Poverty and a Profile of the Urban Poor in Thailand," *Quarterly Review,* Thailand Development Research Institute, Vol. 5, No. 4 (December 1990).

Ingram, James C., *Economic Change in Thailand, 1850–1970* (Stanford, California: Stanford University Press, 1971).

International Monetary Fund, *International Financial Statistics*, various issues.

———, *World Economic Outlook, May 1991* (Washington: International Monetary Fund, 1991).

Jansen, Karel, *Finance, Growth and Stability: Financing Economic Development in Thailand, 1960–86* (Aldershot, England: Avebury, 1990).

Johnson, R. Barry, "Distressed Financial Institutions in Thailand: Structural Weaknesses, Support Operations, and Economic Consequences," IMF Working Paper, WP/89/4 (January 1989).

Makin, John H., "Effects of Inflation Control Programs on Expected Real Interest Rates," *Staff Papers*, International Monetary Fund, Vol. 29 (June 1982), pp. 204–32.

Meesook, Oey Astra, "Income, Consumption and Poverty in Thailand, 1962/63–1975/76," World Bank Staff Working Paper, No. 364 (Washington: World Bank, November 1979).

———, and others, "The Political Economy of Thailand's Development: Poverty, Equity and Growth, 1850–1985" (unpublished; World Bank, 1988).

Pakkasem, Phisit, *Leading Issues in Thailand's Development Transformation, 1960–1990* (Bangkok: National Economic and Social Development Board, Office of the Prime Minister, 1988).

Price Waterhouse, *Worldwide Summary of Individual and Corporate Taxes, 1990.*

Rieger, H.C., "The ASEAN Organization—Where Now?" in *The ASEAN Countries—Economic Structure and Analysis*, Economist Intelligence Unit, Regional Reference Series (London, 1989).

World Bank, *Thailand: Toward a Development Strategy of Full Participation* (Washington: World Bank, 1980).

———, *Thailand: Managing Public Resources for Structural Adjustment* (Washington: World Bank, 1984).

———, *Social Indicators of Development, 1990* (Baltimore, Maryland: Johns Hopkins University Press, 1991).

Recent Occasional Papers of the International Monetary Fund

85. Thailand: Adjusting to Success—Current Policy Issues, by David Robinson, Yangho Byeon, and Ranjit Teja with Wanda Tseng. 1991.

84. Financial Liberalization, Money Demand, and Monetary Policy in Asian Countries, by Wanda Tseng and Robert Corker. 1991.

83. Economic Reform in Hungary Since 1968, by Anthony R. Boote and Janos Somogyi. 1991.

82. Characteristics of a Successful Exchange Rate System, by Jacob A. Frenkel, Morris Goldstein, and Paul R. Masson. 1991.

81. Currency Convertibility and the Transformation of Centrally Planned Economies, by Joshua E. Greene and Peter Isard. 1991.

80. Domestic Public Debt of Externally Indebted Countries, by Pablo E. Guidotti and Manmohan S. Kumar. 1991.

79. The Mongolian People's Republic: Toward a Market Economy, by Elizabeth Milne, John Leimone, Franek Rozwadowski, and Padej Sukachevin. 1991.

78. Exchange Rate Policy in Developing Countries: Some Analytical Issues, by Bijan B. Aghevli, Mohsin S. Khan, and Peter J. Montiel. 1991.

77. Determinants and Systemic Consequences of International Capital Flows, by Morris Goldstein, Donald J. Mathieson, David Folkerts-Landau, Timothy Lane, J. Saúl Lizondo, and Liliana Rojas-Suárez. 1991.

76. China: Economic Reform and Macroeconomic Management, by Mario Blejer, David Burton, Steven Dunaway, and Gyorgy Szapary. 1991.

75. German Unification: Economic Issues, edited by Leslie Lipschitz and Donogh McDonald. 1990.

74. The Impact of the European Community's Internal Market on the EFTA, by Richard K. Abrams, Peter K. Cornelius, Per L. Hedfors, and Gunnar Tersman. 1990.

73. The European Monetary System: Developments and Perspectives, by Horst Ungerer, Jouko J. Hauvonen, Augusto Lopez-Claros, and Thomas Mayer. 1990.

72. The Czech and Slovak Federal Republic: An Economy in Transition, by Jim Prust and an IMF Staff Team. 1990.

71. MULTIMOD Mark II: A Revised and Extended Model, by Paul Masson, Steven Symansky, and Guy Meredith. 1990.

70. The Conduct of Monetary Policy in the Major Industrial Countries: Instruments and Operating Procedures, by Dallas S. Batten, Michael P. Blackwell, In-Su Kim, Simon E. Nocera, and Yuzuru Ozeki. 1990.

69. International Comparisons of Government Expenditure Revisited: The Developing Countries, 1975–86, by Peter S. Heller and Jack Diamond. 1990.

68. Debt Reduction and Economic Activity, by Michael P. Dooley, David Folkerts-Landau, Richard D. Haas, Steven A. Symansky, and Ralph W. Tryon. 1990.

67. The Role of National Saving in the World Economy: Recent Trends and Prospects, by Bijan B. Aghevli, James M. Boughton, Peter J. Montiel, Delano Villanueva, and Geoffrey Woglom. 1990.

66. The European Monetary System in the Context of the Integration of European Financial Markets, by David Folkerts-Landau and Donald J. Mathieson. 1989.

65. Managing Financial Risks in Indebted Developing Countries, by Donald J. Mathieson, David Folkerts-Landau, Timothy Lane, and Iqbal Zaidi. 1989.

64. The Federal Republic of Germany: Adjustment in a Surplus Country, by Leslie Lipschitz, Jeroen Kremers, Thomas Mayer, and Donogh McDonald. 1989.

63. Issues and Developments in International Trade Policy, by Margaret Kelly, Naheed Kirmani, Miranda Xafa, Clemens Boonekamp, and Peter Winglee. 1988.
62. The Common Agricultural Policy of the European Community: Principles and Consequences, by Julius Rosenblatt, Thomas Mayer, Kasper Bartholdy, Dimitrios Demekas, Sanjeev Gupta, and Leslie Lipschitz. 1988.
61. Policy Coordination in the European Monetary System. Part I: The European Monetary System: A Balance Between Rules and Discretion, by Manuel Guitián. Part II: Monetary Coordination Within the European Monetary System: Is There a Rule? by Massimo Russo and Giuseppe Tullio. 1988.
60. Policies for Developing Forward Foreign Exchange Markets, by Peter J. Quirk, Graham Hacche, Viktor Schoofs, and Lothar Weniger. 1988.
59. Measurement of Fiscal Impact: Methodological Issues, edited by Mario I. Blejer and Ke-Young Chu. 1988.
58. The Implications of Fund-Supported Adjustment Programs for Poverty: Experiences in Selected Countries, by Peter S. Heller, A. Lans Bovenberg, Thanos Catsambas, Ke-Young Chu, and Parthasarathi Shome. 1988.
57. The Search for Efficiency in the Adjustment Process: Spain in the 1980s, by Augusto Lopez-Claros. 1988.
56. Privatization and Public Enterprises, by Richard Hemming and Ali M. Mansoor. 1988.
55. Theoretical Aspects of the Design of Fund-Supported Adjustment Programs: A Study by the Research Department of the International Monetary Fund. 1987.
54. Protection and Liberalization: A Review of Analytical Issues, by W. Max Corden. 1987.
53. Floating Exchange Rates in Developing Countries: Experience with Auction and Interbank Markets, by Peter J. Quirk, Benedicte Vibe Christensen, Kyung-Mo Huh, and Toshihiko Sasaki. 1987.
52. Structural Reform, Stabilization, and Growth in Turkey, by George Kopits. 1987.
51. The Role of the SDR in the International Monetary System: Studies by the Research and Treasurer's Departments of the International Monetary Fund. 1987.
50. Strengthening the International Monetary System: Exchange Rates, Surveillance, and Objective Indicators, by Andrew Crockett and Morris Goldstein. 1987.
49. Islamic Banking, by Zubair Iqbal and Abbas Mirakhor. 1987.
48. The European Monetary System: Recent Developments, by Horst Ungerer, Owen Evans, Thomas Mayer, and Philip Young. 1986.
47. Aging and Social Expenditure in the Major Industrial Countries, 1980–2025, by Peter S. Heller, Richard Hemming, Peter W. Kohnert, and a Staff Team from the Fiscal Affairs Department. 1986.
46. Fund-Supported Programs, Fiscal Policy, and Income Distribution: A Study by the Fiscal Affairs Department of the International Monetary Fund. 1986.
45. Switzerland's Role as an International Financial Center, by Benedicte Vibe Christensen. 1986.
44. A Review of the Fiscal Impulse Measure, by Peter S. Heller, Richard D. Haas, and Ahsan H. Mansur. 1986.
42. Global Effects of Fund-Supported Adjustment Programs, by Morris Goldstein. 1986.
41. Fund-Supported Adjustment Programs and Economic Growth, by Mohsin S. Kahn and Malcolm D. Knight. 1985.
39. A Case of Successful Adjustment: Korea's Experience During 1980–84, by Bijan B. Aghevli and Jorge Márquez-Ruarte. 1985.

Note: For information on the title and availability of Occasional Papers not listed, please consult the IMF *Publications Catalog* or contact IMF Publication Services. Occasional Paper Nos. 5–26 are $5.00 a copy (academic rate: $3.00); Nos. 27–64 are $7.50 a copy (academic rate: $4.50); and from No. 65 on, the price is $10.00 a copy (academic rate: $7.50).